'It is Byrne's sense of the ridiculous as well as the sublime that c:
compelling reading.'
In Dublin

'ous and to
V...e

'Byrne records the events of his life with a merciless, moving and
extraordinarily perceptive eye.'
Sunday Independent

'The writing is tinged with poetry. Powerful.'
American Bookseller

'Wistful, beautiful and completely sincere.'
Irish Press

'Delightful. Will have the reader calling for more.'
Publishers Weekly

'Entertaining and moving. Much more than an autobiography. Byrne's
incurable romanticism imbues (the book) with a subtle blend of celebration
and melancholy revealing a talent that is enormous and instinctual.'
Helena Mulkerns

'A great collection of writing.'
Connaught Tribune

'... a hauntingly exciting writer who makes the hairs stand out on your
neck with his graphically succinct style.... He tells it like it is — and was —
in his heady tapestry of dream and memory. This is
a treasure trove, a goldmine. Unputdownable.'
Modern Woman

'The book is alive from cover to cover.
Every chapter is compulsive reading.'
Sunday World

'Compelling and beautifully written.'
Sunday Press

'Byrne's writing conveys the impression of someone whose awareness
since childhood has been blisteringly perceptive
... magical and at times, searing.'
Irish Times

'Byrne is a talker — a glorious talker in that wonderful acerbic,
sentimental, philosophical Irish way. These sketches ... (are) extremely
funny, with a gentle eye for human vagaries and
dialogue that dances off the page.'
Elle

Gabriel Byrne was born in Dublin. He is an internationally acclaimed actor and producer with over twenty films to his credit, including: *Miller's Crossing, The Usual Suspects, Little Women, Into the West* and *Man in the Iron Mask* (actor); *Into the West* (executive producer); *In the Name of the Father* (executive producer, nominated for seven Oscars); *Last of the High Kings* (producer); *Mad About Mambo* (executive producer); *Draíocht* and *Last of the High Kings* (writer).

He has two children and divides his time between Los Angeles and Ireland.

pictures in my head

GABRIEL BYRNE

WOLFHOUND PRESS

This edition published in 1999 by
WOLFHOUND PRESS Ltd
68 Mountjoy Square
Dublin 1

First published 1994

British Library Cataloguing in Publication Data
A catalogue record for this book is available from the British Library

ISBN 0 86327 709 8

Earlier versions of some of these texts were previously published in the following magazines or newspapers and are hereby acknowledged: *Magill, The Sunday Press, Image* magazine. And I scripted and read some of these as 'Reel Memories' broadcast on RTÉ radio.

10 9 8 7 6 5 4 3 2 1

Cover photograph coutesy of Michaels, Wolfe and Tencer
Cover design: Ann W. Douden
Typesetting: Wolfhound Press
Printed in Ireland by Colour Books, Dublin

Contents

For my darling children
Jack and Romy and for Áine

Also to the memory of my sister Marian and my father Dan

Acknowledgements

Thank you to my mother Eileen, my brothers Tom and Donal, and my sisters Margaret and Breda.

Also to Teri Hayden, my dear friend, and Sean Lawlor.

To John McColgan and Moya Doherty, Paul Bennett, Barry Devlin, Caroline Erskine, Brial Palfrey, Shay Healy, George Barkin, John Lennon, Leora Bloch, Eoghan Harris, Anne Harris, Doris Levine, Walter Donahue, Eibhlín Ní Bhroin, Reiltín Ní Bhroin, Máire Garvey and all at 29, the late Mary Murphy, Mary McCarthy, Holy Faith, Glasnevin, Mary Healy-O'Brien, Finglas Girls' School, the Marquis Michael Des Barres, Amy Singer, Patrick Rainsford, Rebecca Moore, Ann McRory, Andrea Eastman, Tracey Jacobs ICM, Noel Ó Briain and Wesley Burrowes.

To Seamus Cashman and Wolfhound.

And finally to two wonderful women who have blessed my life in more ways than they know:
Áine O'Connor whose idea this book was, and
Ellen Barkin, the mother of my children.

Introduction

Once when I was returning from school on the 50B bus, a man got on who caused a 'commotion'. Bus travellers at the time were accustomed to the unpredictable theatre of ordinary journeys as well as to the exits and entrances of many beloved 'actors'. The ones I remember best are Bang Bang who shot people with his finger. We had gun finger shootouts with him on many occasions ducking down behind the seats for cover.

Or Molly Coddle, a girl-woman of about fifty, given to addressing passengers in a loud voice. She'd fix an unfortunate shopper from the television seat: 'Howye misses,' she'd say. 'Did you get it last night? I'd say you did by the look of you! I love a bit meself, that's being honest with yis. Here, what's the difference between a ride and a donkey? — Do yis give up? You can beat a donkey, but you can't beat a good ride.'

The man who caused the 'commotion' everybody seemed to know. He wore a sports coat that was too small for him, and trousers that were baggy and stained. His shoes were scuffed and he wore no socks. The shirt was open at the neck. He sang a song. Everybody gave him a big hand when he finished. He had to get off at Our Lady's Hospital because he said he was going to Crumlin and the 50B went to Walkinstown Cross.

He said goodbye before he got off and people said 'Take care of yourself' and 'Good luck now' and shook his hand as he came down the aisle. The conductor said 'Watch your step there, like a good man.' The driver pushed back his glass door and waited for him to get off, throwing his eyes up to heaven and smiling at the passengers. The man saluted the conductor and said something in Irish. I watched him, as he stood there on the footpath, swaying and still saluting the departing bus.

The conductor clicked his tongue: 'Now! You'd be talking!' and pressed the bell. People started to mumble to each other, turning round to get a last look at him. Then somebody said his name and said it with reverence and affection. For many years afterwards when I heard the word 'writer', that is the image that came unbidden into my head — a man singing, his head to one side, his hand raised in salute and the rain falling on him — Brendan Behan.

—

My first book was *Treasure Island*. How I longed to live at the Admiral Benbow keeping watch for a seafaring man with one leg. Every month I took the *Our Boys* to follow the tales of 'Kitty the Hare' by Victor O.D. Power ('Twas a wild windy night, God bless the hearers ...'). Later I graduated to Dickens and the English classics. I longed to use words like 'jolly' and 'beastly', and was disappointed I could never get away with 'I say you chaps' to members of our gang in Walkinstown!

Then writers like Stan Barstow and Alan Sillito and John Braine became my literary heros. Now I wanted to use words like 'friggin' and 'bint' and say things like 'Bugger this for a game of soldiers.'

Then I read *Goodbye to the Hill* by Lee Dunne. For the first time, I heard a voice that I totally recognised. I loved the simplicity of the writing, the familiarity of the locations — Rathmines in a novel — and, of course, the characters. It was a book about people and streets that we knew, and it was funny and sexy.

Lee Dunne made it look simple. As did Sillito. So I tried to write a kind of Dublin 'Saturday Night and Sunday Morning'. Ah well! I fast came to realise that writing was hard, damned

hard, and with relief abandoned it 'til my mid-twenties at UCD.
Now I was reading Camus, Beckett and all the other fashion-
ably 'in' writers.

A friend, Mary Healy, encouraged me to submit pieces, and
I had a little success on RTE and BBC. But I was more interested
in 'playing' at writing than actually doing it. Drinking pints in
the Bailey and scribbling 'til I was overcome by Guinness. I still
preferred to read — John McGahern, Brian Moore and Edna
O'Brien above all; but also John Broderick, Patrick Boyle, Bryan
McMahon, Ben Kiely, O'Connor, O Faolain, O'Flaherty ...

I attempted to become a journalist, buying a typewriter from
the proceeds of a Friday night pools round. I received no replies
to my badly typed applications, and relinquished my dreams of
glory on Grub St.

—

A few years ago, I returned to writing when Áine O'Connor
with whom I had lived for twelve years forced me to submit a
piece to Anne Harris at *Image*. She in turn encouraged me and
later commissioned further efforts. Somehow John Waters came
to hear of my scribbling and asked me to do a column for *Magill*
(some of those pieces are incorporated here), and their publication encouraged me.

At school I used to write essays for other students experi-
menting with different styles and themes, and took secret
delight in their being read and graded by the teacher. That was
when I most enjoyed writing. Then, my only real ambition in
life was to be Dylan Thomas. After thirty years, his work still
has the power to thrill me like that of no other writer. He is my
all time literary hero.

—

With this book, I set out with no clearer purpose than to let go images that had, as William Trevor says, become 'snagged' in my memory.

In releasing them, I hope the reader enjoys them and identifies and in the process comes to know something of my spirit.

—

Postscript

I am sitting by the Rio Grande. The desert stretches away endlessly. I am making a cowboy picture with two old friends from the Apollo in Walkinstown, Robert Mitchum and Jack Palance. I am still playing cowboys! And the sky seems as blue and innocent as it always did back then. And for just a few moments I can believe that nothing has changed. And that's the magic.

Gabriel
November '94
Santa Fe, New Mexico

A Happy Little Song
in my Secret Soul

We are standing outside the Rotunda Hospital. My mother
and I. In her arms my newly born brother. The wind
slaps his blanket into his face. My mother's hand moves it away.

'Poor baby,' she says. 'You'll get your end.'

I am cold. I stamp my feet to keep warm. We are waiting for
my Uncle Joe to collect us.

'A body could be dead, waiting,' she sighs.

She looks first one way, then the other. An old woman with a
shopping bag looks at my brother. 'Is it a he or a she, missus?'

'It's a he,' says my mother.

'God bless him and long life to him.'

'Do you like your new brother?' she asks.

I hide behind my mother's skirt. The wind makes it flap.

'Are you a shy boy?' says the old woman. When she smiles
her teeth are stained with lipstick, like blood.

'At long last,' says my mother.

Uncle Joe's vegetable van pulls onto the pavement. He jumps
out. He has on his brown work-coat. He runs to the back doors
but he cannot open them. They are tied with twine. 'Jasus,' he
says. He spits his cigarette onto the road. Finally the doors come
free. He turns and smiles.

'About time,' says my mother.

'I can't be in two places at the one time, you know,' says
Uncle Joe. He takes my hand.

My mother looks into the back of the van.

'You're not serious?'

'What?'

'I can't go in there. You don't expect me to go in there on top of the vegetables?'

'Where d'ya want to go, on the roof?' says Uncle Joe.

'Not 'til ye clean up a space. The least you could do.'

Uncle Joe is on his hunkers in the van. There are bags of onions and potatoes and scallions and turnips and tomatoes and sprouts and all kinds. There is also a weighing scales. Uncle Joe takes the baby from my mother. 'Get in first you.'

My mother says 'yuck' as her knee squashes a tomato. She is on her hands and knees. Uncle Joe follows behind. He places my brother on the weighing scales. 'Upsa-daisy,' he says.

'Are you cracked?' says my mother. 'Give me that child before ye kill him stone dead.'

'Jasus, look,' says Uncle Joe. 'He weighs two and a half stone, not even the weight of a small bag. D'ya think he looks like me?'

'Why would he look like you?'

'Well, being brother and sister.'

'Does he look like a dunderhead?'

'Begob he doesn't,' says Uncle Joe.

'Well then, there's your answer.'

'Always the bitter word,' he says.

There's always a queer smell from the back of Uncle Joe's van. The smell of rotten vegetables and fruit. Still I like it in there. Sometimes I help him on his rounds, going round the roads listening to him as he talks to the women who come to buy. In the summertime the flies buzz around in there in the heat. Bluebottles the size of your fist. But today it's cold.

Uncle Joe makes a face in through the window, crossing his eyes. My mother shakes her head and clicks her tongue. Then she smiles over at me.

Uncle Joe slams the door closed, then he climbs into his seat. 'Are we ready for take-off?'

'Just get on with it for God's sake and get us home.'

Through the window I watch the street speed by. Uncle Joe is singing: 'I never felt more like singing the blues and I never thought that I'd ever lose your love babe — ya got me singing the blues.'

When the van stops, we all lurch forward for a moment, then we straighten up. My mother is talking to my brother, smiling, making baby sounds to him. I'm taking the stones out of plums and spitting them to see if I can hit the back of Uncle Joe's head. My mother tells me to stop.

We walk up the garden path. All the neighbours are out for a gawk at my brother and they all think he's the bee's knees.

—

I am looking at my father's face. His face is afraid. He is running from the room shouting for my mother. 'Come here quick.'

'What is it?' she says, running from the kitchen.

'He's after poisoning the baby,' my father says.

They are looking at me. They are angry now. My brother is looking at me from his pram.

'Look — his face — he's turnin' blue,' my father says. My brother wears a pointed pink woollen hat, and the turpentine I've given him to drink is dribbling from his lips. Now they are forcing a spoon into his mouth. There is a smell of vomit. I feel a smack of pain. The little whiskey bottle of turpentine spills to the floor. My father is shaking me. 'What kind of a divil is in you?'

I start to cry. Now I am afraid too. My mother is rocking my brother backwards and forwards in her arms. Now there is a strange man I do not recognise in the room. He has a black bag. He is listening to my father.

'I was just doin' a bit of painting — he must've thought it was whiskey. You can't watch them all the time.'

I like my brother. I like to tickle his feet with a goose feather to see him laugh and kick his legs.

'There's some class of a *mí-ádh* on him, doctor,' my father says, nodding his head at me, 'and this isn't the first time he's done it either. I caught him trying to stuff a lump of turnip down the baby's throat a few weeks ago. Luck of God I came in or — or — he'd have been dead on us.'

The man with the black bag leaves. I sit on the window sill where it's warm. I watch him go down the path. He turns at the gate and waves at me and smiles. I hear my father say, 'Get out of that window, you're worse than an oul' cat. If I ever see you next or near that baby tryin' to give him anything again, I'll bate the lard out o' ye. Now go over there and say you're sorry to your brother — go on, tell him you're sorry.'

'I'm sorry. For tryin' to kill you — I — I didn't mean to.'

My brother makes a gurgly sound in his throat. He is playing with the coloured balls which stretch in a string across his crib. And he smiles at me because he doesn't know I tried to murder him even though I didn't mean it.

—

We live in a house on a road called after a mountain. All the roads are called after mountains. We know them by heart. Errigal, Brandon, Cooly, Ben Madigan, Mourne. All the houses are like our house, only some have different curtains and gardens. The Kennedys have a monkey-puzzle tree. My father says it comes from Africa.

Every day I see Mrs Kennedy walking to the shops. She has a blue coat. Her hair is red. She always smiles at me. Sometimes she gives me choc-ices. She says it's a present for me. She talks over the hedge to my mother. She takes me and my brother for walks. We keep having to stop because he's always throwing things out of his pram. She says he's a heart-scald and laughs. The hood of his pram is up and over his head there is a little picture of the Sacred Heart which blows in the breeze, and a string with plastic giraffes and monkeys of all colours which people are always moving over and back to make him look at. She likes to bring us for walks because she has no children of her own and my father says she's practising for when she has. She calls me her sweetheart. 'Where's my little sweetheart?' she says when she comes to the house.

My father tells her about the time I tried to murder my brother and she says, 'Oh, he'd never do that.'

'Begob he would and he did. Just because he's your favourite.'

One day she brings us to the zoo. My mother comes too. My mother's dress is white with brown spots and we get our photos taken in front of the giraffes. In the picture they look like they have my mother's dress on, my Dad says.

One day my father comes into the front room. My mother is doing the ironing and she is singing to herself. He sits down in Uncle Alfred's chair. For a long time he says nothing. Then he says quietly, 'Peggy Kennedy is dead.'

There is a circle of flowers on the door of the Kennedys' house and the curtains are closed in all the houses of the street. I ask my father why. 'It's a mark of respect for the dead,' he says. The Kennedys' house smells different to ours. The hallway is crowded with people from the road. I am holding my father's hand. All the people are talking low to each other. Mr Kennedy is a soldier. He is sitting by the fire. The flames are shining in his soldier's boots. He holds my father's hand tight. He doesn't look at me. I can't hear what they are saying.

Mrs Kennedy is lying on the bed. I watch to see if she's breathing but she isn't. On the table a candle is burning in the dark room with the curtains closed. Her hands are joined together, like she's saying her prayers.

My father says 'She's gone to heaven.'

Mr Kennedy says 'Yes, she's in heaven.' Then he leans against the wall and turns his face away. My father bends over the body of Mrs Kennedy and he kisses her on the forehead. He lifts me up and I kiss her there too. It is cold in the room with the candle flickering and I hear the rain against the window. I think of her smiling at me and saying 'my sweetheart' and giving me the choc-ice that day.

The men in black coats carry the coffin along the landing and they say, 'that's it — easy now,' because the handles scrape the wall and the stairs is narrow. The handles are bright and silver and the wood has a queer smell from it and all the people follow the long black car with all the flowers on it and it slowly moves away down our road with everybody standing without saying anything and just looking, making the sign of the cross and bowing their heads.

—

It is early morning. Always I wake to hear my father downstairs getting ready for work. He works in the brewery where they make porter. He wears a blue jumper with 'Guinness' written in red letters across the chest and back. He wears a thick black belt with badges on it from when he was in the army, and big boots that he polishes every night and leaves in front of the fire. Where the laces go are little holes that look out at you like eyes. I hear the crackle of the radio and a man with an English accent and music. I hear my father move between the kitchen and the dining room, talking to himself and saying, 'Be the hokey, man'. I sometimes watch him through the bars of the banisters, shaving in the mirror. He never sits at the table to eat. He always stands and leans with one hand on the back of a chair and drinks his tea from a big white mug with 'Guinness' written on it and talks to himself. When he sees me he says 'You'll get your death sitting there.'

Before he leaves, he brings tea to my mother. He sits on the side of the bed smoking and talking to her. Through the walls I can hear them laughing. Then he comes into our room and makes the sign of the cross with his thumb on my forehead and on my brother's. We pretend to be asleep. I hear the door close behind him and the house is silent.

My mother's bed is big and warm. I lie beside her in the early morning and she talks to me. 'I saw the banshee the night before poor Peggy died.'

'What's a banshee?' I ask.

'A fairy woman that follows certain families and cries outside their houses the night before they die. She has long red hair down to her waist and she combs it as she cries. It woke me up, the screeching of her.'

'Whereabouts did you see her?'

'Just below the window there, under the lamp-post, as plain as day. I heard her and I knew there was a death coming. It put the heart crossways in me.'

Every night I lie awake listening for the call of the fairy woman with the long red hair and her comb but I never hear her because only my mother can. You always know when a person is going to die because of the banshee or because a bird flies into the house or if a mirror falls off the wall. She says that before her father died, a strange black bird flew into the kitchen and she knew then as well, just like she did with Peggy. Over the dressing-table there is a picture of Our Lord holding out his hands. They are bleeding from where the soldiers drove nails into them and killed him. He has long black hair like my mother's, and he looks kind and the nails are hurting him but he doesn't seem to mind.

Outside in the street I can hear the milkman whistling and the milk bottles rattling. His horse always stands and waits for him to go into the houses and moves along without being told. The horse's name is Ned and as I lie next to my mother I hear him say, 'Hup Ned'. My mother says, 'There's Ned. Time to rise, time to shine.'

We kneel either side of the bed and I say my prayers to my Guardian Angel to keep me safe from harm. I can't see him but I know he's standing there behind me. He has big white wings and a big white shirt and white hair and his hands are joined and his head is bowed down, listening to me praying to him. Sometimes I look around real quick to see if I can catch him but I never can. We say together:

> Hail Holy Queen, Mother of Mercy,
> Hail our Life, our Sweetness and our Hope,
> To thee we cry poor banished Children of Eve,
> To thee we send up our sighs mourning and weeping.

This is my favourite prayer because I love the words and hear the sound of them and hear my mother's voice saying them too, with her eyes closed and her head bent down, just like my Guardian Angel.

—

We move from our house to another house. It is in the dark. My brother is asleep in the pram and there are pots and kettles and things on top of him. It is raining. Under the light from the street, the rain looks yellow. The lamps of the cars coming towards us make my mother look away. She is wearing her coat with the black and white squares and spongy boots with zips up the front. She has a scarf with horses' heads and dogs on it which is wet and sticks to her head.

We pass over the bridge and I look into the river. It is the Camac. It only goes to Inchicore and Chapelizod but they can smell it in China, she says. In the windows of the houses the lights of the televisions are winking on and off. She is pushing the pram against the wind that comes down from the mountains. The knuckles of her hand are white from gripping the bar of the pram and there is rain stinging our faces. My father is working late because it is coming close to Christmas, so we have to go to our new house by ourselves. The double-decker bus passes down the road full of people all dry and warm inside and rubbing the windows to look out.

I am sad to leave our old house and all the time I keep thinking of the rooms all empty and echoey now and wonder if it's still there and if there are new people in it now. Before I leave I bury a paper gun which I got from the back of a corn-flakes box. It is hidden in a deep hole in the tool shed at the bottom of the garden and I think, will it be there forever or will the new people find it and know I buried it there.

My mother puts the brake on the pram. She goes to open the gate. It is low and made of wood. It has a name on it in white letters nailed to the top. My mother is pulling the bolt back and pushing the gate open. It scrapes along the path. The house is dark and there are no curtains on the windows. The lamp from the street shines into the bare rooms at the front and on the long grass in the garden, and our feet crunch on the gravel path and then we stand in the porch and my mother bends down and puts her hand under the mat and finds a key. The house smells cold and we can hear our voices all around us in the quiet. She feels along the wall and then a light comes on. I look at the walls. There are holes in them. There is no lino on the floor which is covered with old newspapers and the stairs are bare and my brother begins to cry and my mother sits on the stairs to get her breath.

Later, my father and my Uncle Joe arrive with the furniture. I help them carry it in through the rain. Around the table we sit, my mother, father and my Uncle Joe. He is telling us a story about himself.

'There I was, missus, cycling along, minding me own busi-ness, not a bother on me. A lovely day it was. The sun splitting the trees. And then I comes round the turn in the road and what do you think I sees in front o' me — what do you think? A motor car turned upside down in the ditch. Well, says I to meself, this is very peculiar. So I hops down off the bike and creeps up to it, 'cause of course you can't be too careful these days. It could be one of them booby traps, do you know, or bless us and save us, there could be somebody hurted or dead maybe. Well 'n anyways, I can see or hear nothing at first, and then be the Lord Jesus I hear this kind of a moan — *uuuuuuuuuu* — like that you know. Well, I says to myself, there's someone in there all right. So says I "Can you hear me?" "Ohh I can," says she — because it was a girl. "Can you get help?" says she. "I'll do better nor that," says I, "I'll have you out before you can say Jack Robinson." "Is that you — Joe?" says she. "The very man," says I. "Oh thanks be to God!" says she and with that down with me into the ditch and I grab the motor car and I heaves it out onto the road and I stretch out my hand and haul your woman out of the ditch and a lovely slip of a girl she was too, beggin' your pardon Missus. "Oh," says she, "Joe Kennedy how can I ever thank you?" "It was nothing," says I. "Let you get into your motor now and off with you and not another word about it," and with that up with me onto the bike and away with me like the clappers. She's looking at me yet, missus.'

'Begob, Joe,' says my father, 'weren't you the powerful strong man for the size of you,' and he looks at my mother.

She smiles and shakes her head.

We stand in the porchway and wave goodbye to Uncle Joe. He waves his hand out the window of the truck.

Later I lie on the mattress on the floor of our new house and listen to the strange sounds from the street below as the moon and the light from the street-lamp make queer shapes on the walls of my new bedroom.

—

Today is my first day at school. The early morning bus is crowded so we must sit on the television seat. My mother and me. I am dressed in a blue coat and have on grey trousers that come to nearly my knee and new shiny patent shoes. On the coat there is the badge of my new school in the shape of a heart. I am sick inside myself with the fear and I hope that we can stay on this bus forever and never get off. I have never been this far into town before, except once when my mother brought me to Clery's shopping and I got lost and there were all these people standing around me in the street and asking me my name and where I lived and where my mother was. A little bent-over man with a plastic hat and a long coat took my photograph and said, 'There ye are now young fella. Get your mother to come around and collect your photo tomorrow,' and he gave me a card with writing on it. When my mother found me she said I was like the baby Jesus in the temple, in the middle of all the crowds of people.

We get off at the Coombe, just before St Patrick's Cathedral. It used to belong to the Catholics, my father says, but the Protestants came along and took it over for themselves so now it isn't like a real church at all.

We walk towards the school, she holding me by the hand and me dragging behind, not wanting to go. The corridor is long and dark and then we come into a little yard with high windows all around. I see gangs of other boys all dressed the same as me. Some of them are running round playing tig and laughing but others are standing there looking around them and they look afraid like me. I think of my brother at home and the way he was looking at me in my new uniform with his head cocked to one side, with his mouth open as if he'd never seen me before. My mother wets her hand and combs my hair back with her fingers. Inside my coat she has pinned a miraculous medal of Our Lady and a piece of paper with my name and address attached to it, just in case I get lost again, like I did in Clery's.

There is a strange smell coming into the yard. It is the smell of O'Keeffe's, the knackers, my mother tells me, where they kill the animals and chop them up and burn them for glue and things. A bell is ringing slow every few seconds, like the bell for Mass in Walkinstown, but much smaller. There are nuns walking among the boys and putting them into lines. They have black belts round their waists and rosary beads that swing by their sides. Some of their faces are cross and they have pointy hats that come down on their foreheads under stiff black veils. They frighten me, but my mother says I have to go with them because they are my teachers now, and they are going to learn me a lot of things and I'll have a grand time.

But I see one of them coming through a doorway and she has a boy by the ear who is crying and she puts him in a line. All the boys are in line and I see another nun ringing a bell, standing in the centre of the yard. Now she is coming towards us. I try to hide behind my mother's coat but my mother pushes me out and makes me say my name and the nun says, 'Sure only babbies cry, isn't that right?' and I say 'yes' and I want to run away and out the door and be lost forever. I see my mother standing there waving at me and she is talking to another woman and my hand is inside the hand of the nun which is white and cold with blue veins and she smells of disinfectant. When I turn around my mother is gone and I am standing beside another boy in a line who looks at me out of the corner of his eyes.

Then the nun says something and we all go into a long thin room with wooden seats that face a big black desk under a window. The nun is sitting behind this desk and all the boys are now quiet and looking at her. She is writing in a big book and doesn't look at anybody but I can hear the scratching of her pen. She puts the top back on the pen and takes a piece of paper and puts it over the writing and moves her elbow slowly over it. She moves her eyes around the room. The quiet frightens me. All I can hear is the ticking of a clock on the wall. She asks if there are any new boys and I say 'me'.

She stares at me. 'Me?' she asks. 'Who is me? Do you have a name, Mr Me? Stand up when I talk to you.'

I go to stand up and my schoolbag catches in the desk behind me. It takes an awful long time to get it off and my face is burning with shame because they are all looking at me. I tell her my name.

'Speak up, I can't hear you.'

I say my name again. This time she says in a loud voice 'Sister. Sis-ter Mary. When I address you, you answer me in a clear loud voice and you say Sister. Do you understand?'

'Yes,' I say low because I am afraid of her cold voice.

'Can I hear him?' she asks the class.

'No Sister,' they all shout together.

'Come out here,' and with her long finger she calls me to the front of the room. I stand there in front of her. There is a fire burning in the grate and I feel the heat on my legs. On a table there is a statue of some saint with a black face, with a crucifix against his chest and he's looking at me as if he was kind of sorry for me. I feel as if I'm going to wet my trousers from the fright, just like the time I woke up in the thunder. I remember thinking that time that I wish I was our cat, because our cat is not afraid of anything.

'Where do you come from?' asks the nun.

'From Walkinstown, sister.'

'Oh, from Walkinstown,' she repeats, as if that was something bad. 'Would they not take you into a school up there that you had to come all this way? Well?'

'I don't know.'

'You don't know what?'

'I don't know, Sis-ter Mary.'

'Well, we'll soon teach you some manners here. Now sit here in front of me where I can keep an eye on you because you look to me like a trouble maker. What do you look like?'

'A trouble maker, Sister.'

'That's better. Sit down.' The sleeve of her veil brushes against my face and I smell that queer disinfectant smell again.

—

Last night I asked my father why I have to go to school.

'Everyone has to go to school.'

'Why?'

'That's why. When I was your age I had to walk three miles to school and three miles back every day in my bare feet.'

He teaches me to count with apples. 'Now if I put one apple there, and then I put another apple beside it, how many apples have I got?'

'Six.'

'How in the name o' Jasus could I have six apples? You just say the first thing that comes into your head. I have two apples. Two.'

And he draws 2. 1 is a line, 2 is like a swan, 3 is a piggy's tail, and I have to draw the numbers for him on a page, and when I get the right answers, he is glad and says, 'We'll make a scholar out of you yet.'

—

The nun stands in front of my desk, the cross of her beads touches my hand. She is telling us things and I look up into her face. A long black hair grows out of her chin and I keep looking at it and I wonder what it would be like to pull it. She tells us a story and we are to draw the story for her on a page with soft coloured sticks.

'Does any boy know who were the Black and Tans?'

I say 'I do, Sister.'

Then she says 'tell the class like a good man' and I tell her the Black 'n' Tans were the British and they came to Ireland and killed and massacred all the people in their beds and they had no religion or anything. And one time, when my mother was a little girl, she was playing with her sister in Roscommon and the Black 'n' Tans came when they were in the chapel, and they came in with their guns and stood in front of all the people praying, and started to laugh and jeer at them. And one of them came up behind the priest on the steps of the altar and hit him on the head with his gun and knocked him down on the

ground, and he rolled the priest down the steps with his foot
and said to the people that if the Black 'n' Tans found anybody
on the roads after six o'clock, they would kill them stone dead.
Every time my mother would hear the trucks, they would hide
in the ditches till they were gone away. My father said there was
nobody in the world worse than the Black 'n' Tans except
Cromwell because they were all out of the jails of England.

Sister Mary smiles while I am telling her my mother's story
about the Black 'n' Tans and says I am a great lad to know all
that. The story she tells us is about her brother who was a
footballer and he played for a team who always wore red shirts.
Only this Sunday, because the other team wore red, they had to
play with white shirts. In the middle of the game, the Black 'n'
Tans burst into the field where they were playing and shot her
brother dead. Their bullets went into his heart and the blood
covered his white shirt and made it red. 'So you see, boys, my
brother died in the colours of his native county after all, and he
died for Ireland.'

The story is sad and I feel like bursting out crying and I think
of Sister Mary's brother lying on the green grass covered in
blood and the Black 'n' Tans laughing and shooting their guns
at the running people.

When we have our drawing done on the page we have to
bring it to her, sitting behind her desk, and she writes 'very
good' on mine. And smiles at me.

A bell rings and we all stand to say the Angelus and then we
all go out to the yard and I see my mother waiting for me with
all the other mothers, and she wraps me up in my overcoat and
asks me how I enjoyed my first day at school and I tell her about
Sister Mary's brother being killed by the Tans and I show her
my drawing and she clicks her tongue and says 'the poor
woman'.

We stand and wait at the bus-stop outside Massey's Funeral
Parlour and it begins to rain. She makes a little paper hat for me
from a newspaper to shelter me and all the buses go by full with

people. Then we get on the 77, and as a treat we go upstairs and we sit in the back seat, and the conductor says 'Fares please', and my mother says 'One and a half to the cross, please' and he pulls my hair and gives me a bus-roll because it's my first day at school, and I make a trumpet out of our ticket and blow it till my mother has to say, 'Stop it — don't be making such a racket.'

When we get in the house my brother is sitting at the kitchen table and he is getting his dinner from the girl who lives next door. Her name is Bernie and she looks after us when my mother goes to work and when she has to go out anywhere. She puts food on a spoon and then blows it and smooths it out and then puts it in his mouth and tips it down his throat.

I show my drawing to Bernie.

'Jasus, he's a great drawer, isn't he, Missus?' Then she asks me what it is. I tell her and she forgets all about feeding my brother and she says, 'The Lord save us. Well, if he keeps on at this rate, there'll be no stoppin' 'im.'

Bernie works in Urneys where they make the chocolates and she works at night. She has a scarf tied in four knots on her head and she wears a white coat like a doctor's and she goes with a fellow who works in the Brillo Pad factory. She calls him 'me chap' and sometimes 'me fella' and she's always talking to my mother about him. They sit at the table in the kitchen for hours talking and whispering and spelling out words that they don't want me to understand. She says things like 'So, says I, don't talk to me about you know what,' and my mother says, 'I know what you mean, Bernie' and glances at me and says 'but of course that's because you have your —' and then she spells a word I don't know and I can't follow what they're saying anymore.

When my father comes in and sees all the cigarette butts with lipstick on them in the ashtray, he says, 'I see the gramophone was here.'

'Oh, she's harmless,' says my mother.

'Harmless is right,' says my father. 'She'd bore the hole off a crow, the same Bernie.'

—

I wait at the roundabout for my father's bus. I know him even in the dark by his walk as he comes up the road. I run to meet him and he whooshes me up into the air and says 'hoops skalara'. I hold his hand to my face and smell the cigarettes from his fingers and I tell him about my first day at school.

'You'll pass them all out yet, so ya will. You'll be a great scholar. D'ya know what I'm goin' to do now?' he says, 'after ya being such a great boy today? I'm goin' to give you a piggyback, and yourself and meself'll go up to the Cherry Tree and I'll buy you a bottle of lemonade and a packet of crisps for yourself, and maybe a pint for myself.'

And so, up on his back with me, and almost as tall as the chimneys on the houses of our street, we cross the road, hupping between the cars, with my hand around his head and shouting 'giddy-up there. Make way for Roy Rogers and Trigger.' And he snorts like a horse and gallops faster and faster 'til we reach the door of the Cherry Tree.

—

One day at the beginning of summer, when I've been at the Holy Faith for a long time, Sister Mary says that it is the time of year when we make the special altar in honour of our Blessed Virgin. So we must all ask our mammies and daddies for flowers.

My father is in the garden at the back of our house. Down one side is a hedge which tumbles onto next door's wall, and at the other side is a long cage with wire, full of budgies and canaries of all different sizes and colours. My father loves his birds because he says they never give him lip, and often I stand and look through the wire and watch him whistling to them, letting them peck at his fingers. Sometimes they fly around and grip the wire with their claws and I stick my fingers in to see if they'll bite me with their beaks. I help him collect groundsel from along the roadway, and sometimes he lets me change their water. He tells me the story of St Francis of Assisi who gave away all his money and every stick of furniture in his house to help the poor people. And every evening the saint would stand outside his door and give a little whistle, and all the birds would come and sit on his head and on his hands, and he would talk to them and ask them how they were and how life was treating them.

But my brother is afraid of the budgies when I lift him up to the wire to look in at them. My mother doesn't like them either: 'You'd think them old birds were human, the way he goes on about them. Morning, noon and night, he's never out of that old cage. One of these days he'll turn into a budgie himself.'

Anyway, this evening he's digging a hole and beside it is a biscuit box with Jacob's Custard Creams written on the side of it. I stand beside him and he pays no heed to me, just keeps digging and digging. Then he stops, and takes the little box and puts it down in the hole and begins to put the clay in on top of it. There are little worms wriggling around in the new clay, so I take a couple to put in my handkerchief for after.

'What're ya doing, Da?'

He doesn't answer but when he has the hole covered up, he says 'Betty Grable's after dying on me. Just keeled over and dropped dead off the perch. Must've been next door's cat frightened the life out of her. She always had a weak heart, poor Betty.'

When he finishes, we just stand there together, looking, without saying anything at all.

—

In the corner of the garden we sit on a car seat which we found in the dump. The evening sun makes the leather hot and he takes out a cigarette from behind his ear and smokes without saying anything. After a while, I tell him about Sister Mary and how we have to bring in flowers for the May altar. It's lovely here in the garden, just the two of us, only the sounds of the motor cars now and then on the Tallaght road and the birds talking to each other and the blue smoke from his cigarette hanging in the air.

'Them old nuns,' he says. 'If it's not one thing, it's another. Books and clothes and pennies for the missions. They'd have a body out the door, the same nuns.'

Every morning he leaves a penny on the table beside my bed before he leaves for work for the black babies in Africa. I'm saving up to buy one to save his soul. You have to put the penny in a box with a black boy's head on it and when the penny drops down, the boy's head nods and nods to say thanks. Sometimes I drop a coat button in, just to see his head go up and down, but this is a sin and Sister Mary says that boys who do that have to confess it in confession. If you put in enough money, then the soul of the baby in Africa is saved from hell, and they'll go to heaven when they die. Every day we say a prayer for the little pagan babies in Africa who have no religion.

My father takes his pen-knife out of his pocket and we go to the end of the garden and he cuts branches of hawthorn and lays them in my arms. Then he collects some wall-flowers and dandelion and in the kitchen we fill an empty milk bottle with water.

The next day my mother wraps the flowers in silver paper and when I get on the bus a woman says, 'Oh, they're beautiful. I wish someone I knew would bring me flowers,' and she laughs at the man beside her.

I sit there looking out the window and thinking of all kinds of things, like it nearly being the summer holidays, and going to Kildare to my uncle's in the country, and the next thing I know is I've gone past my stop and I have to get off at Dame Street and run all the way back. I've never been late before and I dread having to say to Sister Mary that I missed my stop and have to get the strap from her. If you arrive late for school, she gives you slaps on the hand with her black belt, and she holds you tight by the wrists so you can't escape, and you can hear her teeth grind as she brings the belt down on you with all her force. Then you sit and rub your hands together till little black things come out of your palms to make the pain go away. Once I asked my friend, Wardo, what these black things were, and he said it's because we're all made out of clay, and that when we die we go back to clay again.

Now I'm running through the streets and I have this feeling between my legs which I've never had before, but I want it to go on, even though I'm so scared of being late. The yard is empty and silent and I hear the boys singing out their tables, and I want to run away down the steps and go home and tell a lie to my mother that there's no school today, but I know that she wouldn't believe me.

I push in the door of my classroom and all the eyes of the boys look towards me, even though they keep on singing their tables. Sister Mary does not look at me and I just stand there waiting. After a while she gets up from her table and the chair scrapes behind her and she comes over to me. I have a sticky feeling now on my legs where the lovely feeling was.

'Why are you late?' she says, looking at the clock. 'Do you have a note to explain yourself?' She is looking really hard at me and she moves the ring round and round on her bony finger.

'I forgot my flowers for the May altar, Sister. I had to go back to get them.'

She looks away to the altar of the Blessed Virgin which is in the corner of the room. Our Lady's eyes are looking up to heaven. She is dressed in a blue gown with a white veil and she is standing on a snake with a long red tongue. She is surrounded by beautiful flowers of all colours.

Suddenly I feel a stinging pain in my face and I am falling across the room. 'How dare you? How dare you insult our Blessed Mother with these weeds?' She is so angry, she can barely get the words out. She is stamping on my father's flowers and kicking them around the room and she is hitting me across my head, my back, my legs, with her belt. She is calling me a schemer and a liar, and that she has a good mind to send me to the head nun to get me sent home forever. She tears the silver paper into tiny bits and throws them at me and then she takes me by the hair and drags me across to where Our Lady is, and makes me kneel in front of her and say I'm sorry.

Afterwards she is kind to me, but still she makes me stand in front of the class until the dinner time bell rings. My eyes are hurting. My face pains where she hit me and I have to read out loud from our English book a story about a fox that comes into a farmer's house dressed up as a man and steals all his hens in a sack and cuts their heads off with an axe.

All the time I am thinking of my father with his pen-knife, cutting the hawthorn for me, and pulling up the wall-flowers and shaking the clay from them and putting them so carefully in my arms. I think of Sister Mary lying in her bed in the convent and sneaking into her room with an axe like the fox in the story, and chopping off her head and chopping up her body and putting it in a sack and dumping the sack in a river and watching it sink to the bottom where nobody will ever find it.

All the time, I keep saying to myself, 'Fucking, fucking, bloody, bloody, damn, blast, fuck, fuck'.

Even though I know it's a sin, I don't care and I think that soon it will be the summer and I will be in the country with my uncle and after that I'll never have to come back because in the new year I start at the Brothers in Drimnagh and I'll be happy then. 'Fuck, fuck, *f-u-c-k*, fuck,' I say over and over again, until it becomes like a little song, a happy little song in my secret soul.

Reel Memories

It is an evening in summer. I am at my grandmother's house, sitting opposite her in a huge, winged chair, listening as she plays the button key accordion. Introducing each tune to me as if I were an audience of thousands at Carnegie Hall. Her white hair is tied in a bun and ash falls from her Gold Flake and onto her black dress and between the folds of the instrument.

The window is open and the lovely sound spills out into the darkening street, making people stop to listen and sometimes to smile. And as she coaxes the music, her eyes close in a kind of dream. And when finished she sighs and fastens the worn straps, and talks of the times in Roscommon when she was a girl, and makes me read to her from books with goose-feather markers, and spell out words I don't understand and tells me what they mean. She loves Dickens, and Robbie Burns, and Canon Sheehan and poor old Oscar, and speaks of them as she would of old friends.

Looking back to an evening in the half-light of that room, filled with the smell of lilac from her garden, among the faded photos and framed jigsaw puzzles, and stuffed owls, I know that memory has made all the evenings I spent there become as one. And I know that this was my first theatre, the beginning of my love for darkened rooms where words and image and music had power to move the soul in transports of delight, as the poet says. She loved talking and telling stories and books and music, but most of all my granny loved the pictures.

I remember crossing the park, my hand in her hand as she

took me to the pictures for the first time. We stood for minutes watching the swans on Fairview Lake, but I was impatient to be away, for the thrill of the picture-house was greater than any swan. We waited for the doors to open, behind a sign on the pavement which said 'One shilling'. A man dressed in a red uniform came out and beckoned us and the other people to a glass box. Granny opened her purse and carefully counted out the coins, and received a ticket with a hole in it, which she gave to another man who stood like a soldier in front of two doors. He took the tickets and tore them and gave us back one half and kept the other and looped it onto a piece of string.

From inside the doors I could hear loud voices, but not like the voices of real people, and I started to feel afraid and she looked at me and smiled and took my hand tightly again and said, 'There's nothing to be afraid of. It's only the pictures.'

All around the foyer there were painted photographs of men with thin black moustaches and women with bright red lipstick like my mother. Then the sentry pulled back the door and we were in darkness with the noise of those strange voices all around us. We edged our way along by a wall like blind people, me holding on to her coat for fear, till suddenly in an explosion of blinding colour, I saw before me the bluest sea I could ever imagine, and on it two huge boats with sails, sailing under a vast blueness of sky. I turned my head in terror into her body, and for an eternity of moments I dared not look again. When I opened my eyes I saw a light beam in the darkness and a voice asked for our tickets, as it came toward us. And with her arm around me, we followed the dancing light as it lit our way along the steps, 'til we found our seats and I sat down overwhelmed by the fear and the mystery and the magic of it all. But as the wonder grew, the terror died. And so I came to know the lovely dark womb of the picture-house for the first time.

Now the lights came slowly on from red stars of glass set high above us in the blue roof and around the walls from flickering lamps. And a snowy curtain that folded into silver trees as it slowly fell, covered the sea and the boat and the white writing and the voices.

'Was that a picture granny?'

'No, that was only an old trailer,' she said. Then she gave me a marshmallow mouse and a *Trigger* bar which I broke in two over my knee. And she hoped I wouldn't be afraid of the next picture because the banshee was in it. But so was Jimmy O'Dea and he was great gas.

A girl in a yellow coat came up the steps between the seats with a tray of sweets. And we bought two Toblerones, and she kept one for after and we split the other between us.

And now the curtain of trees was going up to the roof again, and the lights faded 'til I could see only the outline of things. And then nothing at all. Then it began. The first picture I ever saw — *Darby O'Gill and the Little People.*

Time has dimmed the memory of the plot, but I remember the fairies and Jimmy O'Dea and the banshee, charging white and terrifying over the hill. And somebody throwing a lantern at the dreaded thing and as it burst into flames the gasps and screams of the few people who were in the audience. But above all I remember a smiling man and a girl sitting on the edge of a swaying haycart, talking as the music played. Nothing more. But the memory of those scenes has stayed with me always.

When we came out it was raining and the lights from the shops shone in the wet pavements but now I looked at everything as if for the first time. For I knew that something had been born within me. And that the world outside the picture-house would never be quite the same again. That evening she played the accordion as usual but the tune she played from under her fingers was the music from the picture. And as she sang,

> Oh for the days of the Kerry dancing,
> Oh for the call of the piper's tune,

I made of my winged chair a swaying haycart, and that night I slept dreaming of lanterns and silver stars and Jimmy O'Dea sailing the biggest of ships on the bluest of seas.

There've been a thousand and one nights and days spent in picture-houses all over the world since that day. On holidays, on Sunday nights, waiting under the town clock in Ballitore for a man on a bicycle bringing silver cans of film from Athy. The cinema a galvanised dance hall, the screen a white bedsheet stretched between two poles. The seats were benches and kitchen chairs and sofas cost sixpence extra. But there I saw Ford and Hawkes and Hitchcock and once an upside-down ten minute version of *North by Northwest*. I was one of these kids forced at strap point into hired buses by the 'the Brothers' to see *Mise Eire* at the Regal. And, as an eight-year-old altar boy, was moved to tears by *Marcellino*, a Spanish film about a young orphan adopted by the Friars, who, upon giving the crucified Christ some bread and wine, is rewarded with the miracle of the Saviour's hand reaching down from the cross to accept his offering. This experience inspired myself and another altar boy, addicted to drinking altar wine and eating congealed candle grease, to purchase a batch loaf and having removed the heels leave it overnight on the altar in the hope of duplicating Marcellino's wondrous feat. Alas we were disappointed.

I have rowdied in lines of bedlam on Saturday afternoons outside picture-houses all over Dublin for the sixpenny rush. And remember standing with my two jam-jars, the price of admission to the Tivoli in Francis Street.

I have reined in my horse at the Apollo in Walkinstown and galloped up Bunting Road dar-darring at any doggone gun-slingin' critter who crossed my path. Have watched with envy the linking lovers pass under the street lights on their way to the forbidden evening shows. The cocksure hair-oiled boys in their gouger's shoes and Elvis suits and their mots click-clicking in slingbacks always just a step behind, leaving the sinful smell of the perfumes in the air for a glorious second. Sat behind them in the balcony, watched and listened in the dark to the sounds of their kissing and tapped them on the shoulders to ask them for a light. Until I got myself a mot of my own, a frail, dark-haired, convent girl, who loved Fabian, Salmineo, Ricky Nelson and me in that order. And I hung up my gunbelt forever, and my whinnying horse was heard no more in the streets of Walkinstown.

—

A procession of long limousines with their blacked-out windows sleeked to a halt outside the Broadway cinema for the New York premiere of Brian de Palma's film about Al Capone and Elliot Ness — *The Untouchables*. A score of spotlights lit the sky over the tall buildings and crowds pushed against the police barriers, straining to catch a glimpse of the stars as they arrived. A red carpet stretched from the sidewalk to the foyer. And each of the celebrities stood for a second and smiled and waved to the cheering crowds before disappearing into the cinema.

The star who was last to arrive, smiling, graceful and now many years older, was unmistakable. The man from the swaying haycart all those years ago in *Darby O'Gill and the Little People* — Sean Connery. And among the flash bulbs and screams and the honking horns of Broadway as he walked away I stood among the crowds, remembering a distant day in Dublin sitting beside my Granny chewing Toblerone as she shared with me her love of the pictures.

Most of the cinemas are gone now, those magic factories of our childhood. The Rialto, The Star, The Leinster, The Tivoli, forever silent. Last Christmas, I passed the Apollo for the first time in years. It was closed and boarded over, the roof torn off and its skeleton of rafters showing in the sky. But the memories remain forever. Real memories of happier, more innocent days before we came to know the world.

But they are always with us, running parallel to the present, shining like stars in a cup of water, as some poet said. Lighting up no path, but never going out.

The End of Summer

My friend Christy and I shared a lot — acting and the theatre and films. As kids we would charge up the Walkinstown Road beating our backsides raw pretending that we were the Durango Kid. We were always falling off walls, seeing who could die the best. Christy was a great dier, and I was really only in the ha'penny place when it came to that. But I was good at being Sterling Hayden in *Terror in a Texas Town* with a straw in my mouth and a kind of bandy-legged walk because of my gun-belt.

Soon we had a gang. Every Saturday afternoon we would go to the Apollo or the Star. We loved cowboys and gangsters and we hated films about animals or girls and most especially we hated kissing. When a coupled kissed we would boo the screen and hiss and stamp our feet and shout 'cut, cut.' And the manager, whose name was Baldy, or Hitchcock sometimes because of his resemblance to Alfred Hitchcock on television, would come down the aisle and shine his torch and get really angry, and then we would all start to sing the Hitchcock theme 'Da, de da, de da da, da da, de da da' and that would drive him nuts altogether. He made us sit two in a seat at the matinee.

There was always a following-upper, which is a kind of serial about somebody, like the Thunder Riders or Batman and at the end of each episode something terrible is always happening to the chap or his mot. Like he's falling out of a skyscraper and then the next week he's not even falling but he's punching the guy we saw pushing him last week. And we always go for it, like eejits.

However Christy was very good at playing girls, and in our gang games he was always the girl, even though we tried not to have them in it. But sometimes, like in the film about the fellow who gets captured by the Germans who tried to get information out of him, they send a girl — well that would be Christy. And he would put on his sister's cardigan and he'd slink up to you and rub your shoulders with his hands and say like a girl, 'so pretty boy, aren't you going to tell your little Mimi where the guns are?'

Walkinstown at that time was on the edge of the country. From the cross, a road wound away to the mountains and the tiny village of Tallaght, among green fields and farmyards that smelled of wet grain and mangolds. There were cows in the fields and ruins of houses from years before and blackberry bushes and the dump where a man called 'The Gull' lived among the rubbish and the old prams and the seagulls. There were piebalds that we rode bareback through the frightened streets and hay wisps in the hedges and the cocks of hay the farmers brought home with horses. The sound of the iron wheels on the roadways and us kids perched carefully on top, kings of all we surveyed. And mothers coming to the doors with their hands to their mouths when they saw us pass and saying, 'sweet mother of Jasus, get down off of there before you end up in Our Lady's.'

The girls in the Urney factory with their smocks and Urney's name written on them, and their hair under their four-cornered-handkerchiefs. Throwing left-overs into the gardens to Christy and me and my brother, and us all with diarrhoea for days and my father saying, 'now youse know what "Any time is Urney time" means,' which is what they used to say on the radio.

And the road was always a theatre of characters. The Jewish men with their long black beards and homburgs carrying their silver cans for milk from Patsy Kavanagh's farm. The strongman who slept in a canvas tent with his dog at the side of the road. A small thick-set man like a bulldog who ate nails and swallowed fire and burst out of straitjackets, and always walked fast with his head down speaking to nobody.

There was the sackman who lived in the shadow of Timmons' Castle which stood like a single rotting tooth just beyond the hill of the Cuckoo's Nest. He was dressed from head to toe in tailored sacks that read 'Boland's Flowermills'. Over his shoulder he carried a bag which we were told contained bold children that he was taking home for his supper.

Three tinkers who rode bicycles without saddles at break-neck speeds known as the 'Bottom Boys': they would career through the Greenhills Road shouting 'hoops skilara' and waving their brown darby hats in the air: the tinker-woman who called looking for 'something for the little baby, Mam, God bless you and save you, God help us, any oul thing at all, or 'e're a copper for a bit ta ate'.

Insurance men and pools men and men selling *Encyclopedia Britannicas*. The monk from Tallaght who would knock you down with politeness, tipping his hat to my mother, looking for loose change. Travelling salesmen with brown cases containing perfumes and nylons and crucifixes and knitting needles and all manner of fancy goods.

Once there was a promotion in the carpark outside The Cherry Tree. Half of Greenhills Road was gathered around a huge red Opel Admiral car. The word spread that somebody famous was inside having a drink with Paddy Whelan. We waited for ages but nobody came out so at last we went home. The next day my mother told us it was Dicky Rock and all the girls on the road were making shows of themselves shouting 'Spit on us, Dicky.' On the way home from school we would stare in the window of the American cleaners at a red-haired girl in a yellow coat who was going out with one of the 'Harmonycords': later they became 'The Bachelors', a famous pop group. Jimmy Bartley, the actor, lived in Crumlin and he was famous because he played a character called Sean Nolan on *Tolka Row*. All the girls, including my mother and Bernie, said that he was a fine thing and they wouldn't mind a slice, whatever that meant.

One day a long black car with flags on it and motorcycles in front and behind came up our road and stopped at the cross. I caught a glimpse of a man in black with a long white face and a black hat leaning on a stick. He looked like he was dead and somebody had propped him up, beside him was a tiny doll of a woman who looked dead too, also in black. That was the president, Mr de Valera and his wife. Both staring out different windows in the rain. We waved but they didn't see us. He was blind as a bat, my mother said.

Then there was the soldier who every week passed our house on his way to the mountains, carrying a gun over his shoulder to shoot rabbits. He wore a long brown coat, winter or summer. People said he was a survivor of the Niemba Ambush in the Congo in 1960, when the Irish troops were massacred by a tribe called the Balubas. Only a few of them escaped. The whole country was in mourning for them.

My father took us out to the Long Mile Road and we stood in silence with the crowds of people as their coffins went slowly past from the airport at Baldonnell. I knew all the soldiers' names and their faces from the photographs in the papers and I repeated words to myself like platoon and cortège and gun carriage and massacre and tricolour and they sent a cold shiver through me.

One day we followed the soldier and his dog and watched as he made off through the fields, 'til he came to a stone between two trees. He sat there for hours looking out toward the mountains, smoking, talking to himself, patting his dog, never touching his gun which lay beside him. Then as it grew dark, he turned back and headed down the Greenhills Road again. People watched him from behind curtains but he never looked in at the houses or tried to see into the rooms, like a lot of people did.

And then he just stopped coming. It took a few weeks to notice but one day Christy said that it was ages since we'd seen him. Then we were on the lookout for him but he never came back again, and for months afterwards we thought about him and waited for him at the cross and wondered where he went with his sad face and his loping walk like he was climbing a hill and his little dog trotting behind him.

One of our teachers was a man called Jerome O'Shea who was full-back for Kerry, he wore a blue suit and he had a quiff of blond hair. Once in the classroom he showed us how to punch a ball out of the square and he almost put his fist through the window. The day after Kerry won the All-Ireland, the Brothers made us all cheer and clap as he stood on the roof of the bicycle shed and the wind blew his trousers and his quiff and he waved to us like he was Billy Furey and not our teacher at all. And we did, even though we were all jackeens and he was from the country.

Every morning before school we loitered with intent within the sweet-shop, presided over by the sweet ladies, Annie and Fanny, identical twins of uncertain age. They moved about among the bulls-eyes and Allsorts and cream pies on stiletto heels in a cloud of perfume. They wore their blond hair piled high on their heads in a beehive style. Their fingernails were pink daggers and their behinds were sweet-apples of sin in stretched slacks. How we lusted after them as we made them sashay sinfully for our purchases. They knew our game of course and took no guff from us for they knew that we loved them, the candy sisters of all our demon boyhood thoughts.

Because I had exhibited a facility for messing about on my father's button-key accordion I was sent to learn the instrument at the school of a noted music teacher in Crumlin called Mr Heaslip. He was an elderly gent of fearsome countenance with little patience. Beneath the fierce glare of a stuffed owl on the piano, he taught me how to play with tentative nail-bitten fingers a host of Irish tunes such as 'Kelly the Boy from Killane' and 'The Rose of Aranmore'. Within a year I had reached such a degree of proficiency that I secured a job as an entertainer in a pub beyond Tallaght, frequented by men who came down from the mountains and stood mournfully looking from them as they endured my often tuneless repertoire. For this I was paid two shillings and all the Lucozade and crisps I could consume.

Within three months I had managed to save four shillings and as a result of reclining between shows on the bed of the proprietor, had infested our house with a plague of enormous fleas which multiplied in number by the day.

My father would often collect me after these appearances. And we ventured down the Tallaght Road unsteadily on his bicycle, he talking to himself and to me now and then, and I clutching for dear life onto the hated instrument.

I was the laughing stock of my friends who came to hear of my instrumental choice. They all had fingers skinned to the bone practising Hank Marvin's *How to play the guitar in two days*.

But Mr Heaslip told me I'd never be on Céilí House if I didn't practise. One day I pushed open the door of the toilet and found him seated on the pot buttering a slice of Procea bread. 'Get out, and have the decency to let me finish my tea in peace!' he shouted.

None of our houses had television and so we used to gather at night-time around the window of the TV shop and watch a black and white picture through the glass on a seventeen-inch Bush screen. In a way it was like going to the pictures except you didn't have to pay in. The only problem was nobody ever knew what was being said behind the glass but there was always a commentator. 'Now that gazebo with the beard is Castro, an awful bowsie altogether, he's from Cuba. And the baldy fella, shouting his head off, that's Kruschev, he's from Russia. You see these two are in cahoots against the Yanks. There's going to be a barney there, mark my words.'

We were always being sent for messages written on the backs of cigarette packets. Mr Garven was the butcher, or the

Victualler as his sign said. His teeth were long and yellow and two pointed ears protruded from his bald head. We called him Lucifer because he looked like a drawing I had seen in a book about the devil. The floor in the shop was covered with sawdust and the marble counter was cold to the touch: a sign behind him read 'Pleased to meet you, meat to please you', and a trio of fat pigs in trousers and waist coats smiled down on us from a shelf. People said that he stuffed his sausages with cat food and horse meat and that he had chopped up his first wife and made rissoles out of her.

Beside us lived Bernie and her sister and her mother, the Wid, which is short for widow. She had a nobbly stick to chase us with and she wore a pair of glasses with one glass covered with an elastoplast. When we were really small she would play horsy with me and my brother pretending each of her legs was a horse and she would bounce us up and down and make us promise not to gallop if she fell asleep. Then she would pretend to fall asleep and make her legs gallop and then pretend to wake up and ask us if we were galloping. And she used tumble us into the deep tent of her skirt when we didn't expect and say, 'up we go and down we go as the gravedigger said.' Often she used to sing us songs that had no words except pretend words like deddle diddle, deddly idle diddle diddle dom. She called us names like heartscalds and nudgers and guarlyas and the bee's nees and the cat's whiskers, alana and pups and black-guards and hareum skareums and say that we took the biscuit and the tin hat. She told us she was a monkey's uncle and the sun of a gun and that her timbers were shivering, but the Wid was the kindest old lady in the whole wide world.

—

One day my brother, who likes to dig holes in the garden because he wants to make a tunnel to go to Kildare to my uncle's house, throws a stone at me, I throw one back at him. It hits him in the forehead. Blood pours from the wound in a crimson river. I am terribly afraid, again. My mother brings him to Our Lady's Hospital and they put stitches and iodine, which leaves a big yellow stain, on his forehead. Later he sits across from me eating ice-cream at the table, my mother between. 'It will have to stop. Youse are worse than the Balubas for fighting.'

And then she starts to say a poem. Nobody can recite a poem like my mother.

> O call my brother back to me
> I cannot pray alone.
> The summer comes with flower and bee,
> Where is my brother gone?
> A rose's brief bright life of joy
> Such unto him was given
> But I must pray alone my boy
> Thy brother is in heaven.

By the end my brother and I are crying. I do not want him to be gone in the summer time or any other time. I realise at this moment that I love my brother and that he loves me, and I vow to let him sleep at the top of the bed from now on. Forever if he wants.

—

We wait at the bus-stop on the Long Mile Road. Our father holds our hands. In the distance we can see the blue sign turning round and round on the roof of the Volkswagon building. At night we can see it from our bedroom going round and round in the darkness. We often lie there watching it, wondering what makes it turn. Now and then lights of cars from the Ballymount Road shine through the trees and throw the shadows of the branches across the room. It always seemed so very far away, that sign. Now we are next to it because from behind that sign comes the bus for the country. It is called the Graiguenamanagh bus and it will bring us to our uncle's house in Kildare for the summer holidays.

I cannot pronounce its name so I call it the grey banana. 'Look dad, dad, here it comes — the grey banana.' I'm always the first to see it, the single-decker green bus, the canvas on the roof flapping in the wind.

The bus comes to a stop. The doors squeal open and Johnny the conductor, cigarette in his mouth, helps us on. We race to the back seat to wave goodbye to our father, who gets smaller and smaller 'til soon we cannot see him any more.

At the Hideout in Kilcullen, Johnny has a pint and he buys us crisps and we look at the withered arm of Dan Donnelly which rests in a glass case.

'Now tell me this,' says Johnny, 'who was the last man to box Dan Donnelly?'

'I don't know,' I reply.

'Give a guess now.'

'Em, John Sullivan,' which was the only boxer's name I knew.

'Get out of that. The last man to box Dan Donnelly was the undertaker,' he wheezes with laughter.

In the town's square we climb down from the bus. Paddy Finnegan the hackney waits for us wearing a hat like a gangster. He brings us to the car. The door is opened out. The inside smells of leather. He talks in the mirror to us. 'The jackeens,' he says and laughs. People watch in doorways as we pass, they wave at us, the gangsters in the back from Dublin.

—

We know the road so well. Every turn and dyke and tree and house and who lives there. I have dreamed of the place at night and every day at school. I feel as if I am going home. My uncle and aunt come from the house. Her hands are covered in flour.

Smoke curls from the chimney behind.

'There ye are,' my uncle says. Silence.

The call of rooks in the trees, the lowing of cows, the dog nosing up to us to see who we are because he's forgotten. Inside the smell of bread baking, twigs and turf burning. The red lamp of the Sacred Heart, the two sad China dogs each side of the clock ticking. A hen being shunted out. My uncle's vest hanging to dry over the fire. The photographs of us all dicky bird watching on the mantlepiece. Shadows on the walls and firelight in the polished shoes and the uncle poking at the embers and asking us how is our mammy and daddy and all belonging to us and how is school.

'Ye have to learn your books: that will stand to ye when ye go out in the world. And did ye meet anyone in the bus, anyone ye like other than yourself?'

We lie in the bed beside the window feeling the small wind in our faces. They are talking low in the kitchen, the radio with news reports from our correspondents. The opening of a door, the crunching of feet on the gravel and the bicycle lights zigzagging out there in the dark and the creaking of a gate, then silence again. My uncle gone to the pub.

We are the boys of summer, browned by sun, stung by nettles, filled with excitement to be in this place of constant wonder. Walking with my uncle, teaching me how to smoke Wild Woodbines in the wet fields of an evening. The clouds low and heavy above.

—

'The end of the world is coming,' he said once as we went to bring home the cattle, and I believed him. And that night as we prayed the Rosary, I asked God not to let the world end until it was time to go back to Dublin again. I prayed that I might be a calf in the field when that happened. 'Do ... do calves go to heaven?' I asked him.

'Oh heaven is full of cattle,' he said. 'That's what I'll be, so,' I said. And so the summer went on — trailers with hayseeds blowing in our eyes, being like men, staggering under forkfuls of hay, sweet tea and currant cake for lunch in the fields, my aunt in her spotted apron leaving a trail behind her in the barley like a boat makes in a sea. And evenings of stories by the fire of headless horsemen and dead relatives that come back to walk the night. Ragwort that turns into fairy coaches and flies to the rath where the fairies live among gold and silver planning to thwart the humans.

Walking home in the star-filled night on the lonely roads with the trees like hands above us, my uncle told me that ghosts were everywhere and that spirits were walking with us. And indeed they were.

'You can go to the pictures if it stops raining,' my aunt said. And all day long it teemed on the laurels at the back of the house and in the garden of bamboo in front, covered Kippley's Hill with a veil and hammered on the galvanised roofs, ran in rivers and ditches and dykes, and all my prayers could not make it stop.

Sometimes on the stillest day we heard like thunder the guns in the Curragh far away, and always the sound reminded me that summer would soon end and that we would return to school, brothers and leathers and sticks and fear.

Then one day my father would come, walking the seven miles from Athy station if the evening was fine. We'd be waiting for him on the road's turn, hear his whistle before we'd see him and run to him. And the buttons of his coat scraping on my face as he hugged us, the sweet bitterness of knowing that at last the summer was over.

Chosen Few

U nder the light from the street lamps we were going into
extra time in the 1963 FA Cup Final and Manchester
United were trailing Leicester City by four goals to three, when
our keeper Deco, a fearless acrobat on concrete or grass, was
called in by his mother.

He had just soared into the light and brought down a dangerous corner ball when she appeared in the doorway.

'Ah Deco,' we begged, 'leave the ball. We're in extra time.'

He ignored us. It was not unusual for our FA Cup Finals or
even World Cup Finals to end thus.

As always, the rest of us repaired to Mario's for a post-
mortem and chips. Then the talk was Elvis and girls and
Brother M, our terrifying teacher of Irish, who'd had a brain
operation and as a result now read everything upside down.

We recognised the priest instantly as he passed the chipper
window. We watched as he stood outside my house checking
the number.

'Jazes, he's going in your gaff.'

Within minutes my brother burst through the door of the
chipper, breathless from running and excitement. 'You've to
come in, you, there's a priest looking for you.'

The priest was sitting in the sofa by the window, drinking tea
from the special occasion china.

'I'm Father Finnerty,' he smiled. 'You remember me, don't
you? You filled in my form when I gave my wee speech the
other day at your school.' He took a Marietta from a plate and

broke it carefully in two like a host.

'Sit down, sit down like a good man. I won't take a lump out of you.' He smiled and peered at me over his glasses. 'So you'd like to be a priest?' he asked.

I remembered him standing under the map of the world in our classroom and, with the geometry ruler, pointing out all the places where his order had missions. Trinidad and Tobago, Liberia, Sierra Leone, Ecuador, Bolivia, Peru, Brazil and Papua New Guinea. I repeated the names silently to myself, over and over in my head like a little poem. Names full of mystery and magic that set the pulse racing with excitement and danger.

He passed a book of pictures around the class. Two boys, suitcases in hand, were opening a gate which led to a lake surrounded by trees. The boys standing on steps being greeted by smiling priests in front of an ivy-covered building: the boys playing snooker and soccer and music. Then a photograph of seminarians, older now, studying in their own rooms, a crucifix behind, the shelves lined with books, sunlight streaming through the windows. Then, a man blessing his proud parents on the day of his ordination and, finally, the same man in shirt-sleeves and a straw hat sitting on a horse surrounded by smiling black children in the shadow of a cloud-topped mountain.

'O yes, Father. I'd like to be one all right.'

'And tell me now, why would you like to become a priest?'

I thought for a moment of myself on a horse in Papua New Guinea in a straw hat. 'To save souls, Father.'

'You have a vocation to the priesthood. Do you know what the word means, "vocation"? From the Latin *vocare*, to call. God is calling you,' he said, breaking another biscuit. 'And you must answer that call.'

I looked at my father. He looked away.

In the porch, Father Finnerty put on his hat. 'God bless you all,' he addressed the entire family, 'and remember, many are called but few are chosen, and a priest in the house is a blessing from God himself.'

We never saw him again.

That night I lay awake, dreaming of villages of straw, fire-red suns, rivers of crocodiles and snake-infested jungles. And me astride my horse galloping brave and reckless to bring salvation to those who knew no God. Oh yes, I would be a priest all right. I was being called. I knew it now.

Crossing the convent field Christy asked, 'Are you really going to be one?'

'Yeh, I am.'

'My oul' fella says you're mad. What about the street leagues?'

'What about them?'

'When are you going?'

'September.'

'Where do you have to go to?'

'A place near Birmingham. Some English gaff. I can't pronounce it.'

'For how long?'

'Seven years.'

'But why do you want to be one?'

I thought for a moment. 'Because many are called but few are chosen.'

'But you're only twelve. You have to be old to be a priest.'

'That's why I'm going to a novitiate, so's I can learn how to say Mass and give communion and hear people's confessions. And then I have to go out to Papua New Guinea to convert all the pagans out there. You can come out and visit me.'

'You have your glue,' he said and walked on.

A clothing list arrived: two grey flannel trousers, black blazer with crest of eagle soaring, six white shirts, three pairs of black shoes and two caps also with crest. I was measured and fitted in Dennis Guiney's of Talbot Street, and then for a gaberdine in Clery's. My mother stitched my number, 558, on to all my clothes. I looked in the mirror and saw a stranger in stranger's clothes and turning the white collar to the front gave myself an apostolic blessing.

The night before I left we had a farewell party. Uncle Joe 'at everybody's insistence' sang his favourite 'Goodbye Johnny Dear'.

> *Don't forget your dear old mother far across the sea.*
> *Write a letter now and then.*
> *And send her all you can.*
> *And don't forget where e're you roam*
> *That you're an Irishman.*

My Auntie Mary was helped from the room in tears, the worse for several bottles of Mackeson's Milk Stout.

'Sure he's only a trawneen. He'll be et alive beyond. O why couldn't he join up with the Brothers at Blackrock?'

'Tis G - G - God's will, Mrs,' stammered Father Clery who had me put out of the church for laughing during the Stations of the Cross.

Evening darkened over Dún Laoghaire. A man on the quay-side, head rocking from side to side like a metronome, played an accordion, and the Legion of Mary handed out leaflets to people as they stepped on the gangplank. Gulls wheeled and bickered over the mail boat and a cold wind swept along the docks. I waved goodbye to my family and friends and stood and watched till the spires and roofs and hills of Dublin became only a line that joined the sea and sky.

Downstairs in the cafeteria, I joined my new friends, my fellow seminarians, all my own age, all dressed identically. In charge of us was an older, flaxen-haired boy from Cork. We sat around him, a flock of frightened crows.

'I am your guardian angel,' he announced, 'and you are my chicks. That's what ye're known as in yeer first year. Ye will all be under my wing till we get beyont.'

The boat thudded and heaved through dark waters. A nun vomited politely into a paper bag, the white of her veil framing her face in the darkness. She staggered away holding the rail like a drunk. A necklace of lights was strung around Holyhead as we slowed towards shore. Disorientated from sleeping only fitfully on the wooden deck benches, we trooped in a line behind our leader, hauling our cases through customs, past Welsh bobbies, stern-faced and reproving under their bizarre helmets. They're not like real policemen at all, I thought.

The doors of the long red train were open and it snorted, anxious to be away from the crowded platform. Soon we were hurtling through Wales, the blackness broken here and there only by a light from a house in the mountains, and all the towns were sleeping now. But once I thought I saw or dreamed I saw a solitary figure stand and wave to our speeding train. I waved back anxious that he should know that I answered his lonely salutation. Our 'guardian angel' rose from his seat and removed the bulb from the ceiling.

'We will all kneel and say the rosary for our Blessed Mother to deliver us safe.' In the darkness I heard his beads rattle. 'I've always had a great devotion to our Blessed Lady myself and of course to Dominic Savio, the patron saint of young boys, so I have.'

He began to intone the first joyful mystery and we answered in half-hearted unison, but my mind made its own prayer to the rhythm of wheel on track: I want to go home, I want to go home, I want to go home.

Later a megaphoned voice announced that we had arrived at Crewe station. A black porter was sweeping the deserted platform. I had never seen a coloured person before.

A light snow was falling over the tracks and on the roof of the train, as we followed our leader from our compartments.

'Right, boys, off with yeer overcoats.' He stood before us in shirt and tie for a moment and then began to jump up and down clapping his hands over his head with every second jump. People watched from the carriage, rubbing the windows. They pointed at us and laughed. I was heartsick with shame and regret.

Snow was falling heavier now, blown by the wind, like a

scattering of wild, white insects beneath the platform lights. Finally we picked up our sodden coats and followed him back to the train. There was some snow on his eyebrows and head, as he settled himself against the seat.

'Now I bet ye're the better of that,' he said.

Dawn whitened the sky as we pulled into New Street station, Birmingham. In a café near the bus terminus we devoured fried bread and eggs and mugs of warm tea. A waitress collected our money, throwing back the Irish coins.

'It's getting up grand now, thank God,' our Guardian Angel said.

'I don't know where you've come from, my love, but this is the worst frigging winter in living memory.'

He ushered us to the door. 'Goodbye now and thanks very much. That was a grand bit of breakfast.'

She turned her back and did not reply.

Through the dismal streets of Birmingham our bus inched its way. Take Courage, a sign on a beer hoarding announced. 'I will, I will,' I said to myself.

Now the city gave way to a sheeted landscape of chocolate box houses of black timber and stone. At last we reached a village, a strange, silent place with names I would never forget, Uriah Crump and Son, Undertakers, The Barley Mow Inn, Mrs Turnbull's Tuck Shop, Bullock's Café. They seemed to me as bizarre as anything Dickens would have invented.

We started walking and soon we passed a graveyard where a woman tending a grave stared at us for a few minutes and returned to her work shaking her head in amusement. A lorry appeared in the distance. Half without hope, I extended my thumb. It halted.

'Who stopped that lorry?' snapped Guardian Angel.

I felt a coward's relief as we clambered, cases and all, into the back.

The gates of the seminary opened to reveal a frozen lake I recognised from the photographs. The branches of trees that edged the ribbon of road that led to my new home were traced in silver. Birds cried in alarm and rose up from the bare trees and only the soft sound of our footsteps followed us. I felt no excitement, only fear and an aching loneliness, and thought how different it all seemed to the photographs passed from desk to desk that day at school. Suddenly, a huge, yellowed building, bearded with ivy, loomed before us. It seemed to possess a dark personality of its own that resented the intrusion of strangers.

There were no smiling priests to greet us. Instead, we waited like the horseman in 'The Listener' as the knocker echoed deep within the house. The door swung open and a small priest with glasses, in a stained soutane, stood before us. I noticed he was wearing Chelsea boots.

'Ah,' he laughed, 'the Irish Brigade.'

We followed him through dark statued corridors, up stairways of uneven stone, hung with paintings of ascetic, long-dead priests. The air smelled of boiled cabbage and disinfectant. Somewhere a piano was being played.

He showed us our dormitories. No bookshelves here, no sunlight streaming through windows, only rows of narrow beds with red woollen covers, our numbers sellotaped to the frames. Around the walls, wooden lockers with your name and year.

Later in the refectory hundreds of boys sat around long tables. One of them was reading aloud from the New Testament in an English accent. On a raised dais three priests sat. Then one of them, removing his napkin from a silver circle, said something in Latin and we were allowed to talk. A wave of noise drowned the silence. When the meal was finished all the Irish boys had to stand and we introduced ourselves amongst clapping and whistles and banging of spoons on the tables. Some of the English repeated our names to each other and laughed. The priest rang a small bell on his table to quieten them.

Before the sacred tabernacle in the flower-filled candle-lit chapel we sang 'Soul of My Saviour', the windows open to the night.

'You are embarking on a most difficult journey. You have chosen a narrow, dangerous road. Temptations will be many. Some of you will not reach the journey's end,' the rector told us from the altar. I glanced at our Guardian Angel. His mouth was tightened in a smile.

'Discipline and prayer and work will be your companions. They will be your strength. For you are now members of a special family and you must turn your back on the empty pleasures of this world, the better to serve Him.'

I thought of my girl in her purple coat, her lovely face smiling at me across the table in the chipper. Irene, my first love from Drimnagh. Must I turn my back on her forever? The boy beside me wet himself, a stain spreading on his grey flannel trousers.

At the entrance to the dormitory, a priest stood reading his breviary in the half light. We extended our hands to show we had washed. He waved us in one by one without a word.

I lay in my thin bed as the lights were extinguished. I listened to the new sounds. The clearing of throats, the whispered conversations, the breathing of sleep, the creaking of springs. Moonlight slanted white over the beds and the stone floors and somewhere a bell rang slow and lonely. I heard the swish of a soutane as it brushed the floors between the beds and the squeak of his shoes in the shadows. A boy cried out in his sleep. All was quiet again.

Sleep would not come for hours, but when it did it was dreamless and deep, 'til I was woken by the sound of bells again. I knelt on the cold floor to pray in my Clery's cotton pyjamas but I could find no prayer, only thoughts of Irene and the roundabout and Mario's one and ones with loads of salt and vinegar, and Mr Goodshow from the paper shop saying 'good show' as he gave you your change and Uncle Joe singing, on an evening that seemed so long ago now, his head thrown back, and the firelight in his whiskey glass.

My seminary life ended after four years. Having been expelled for the crime of smoking in the graveyard, I was dispatched shamefully back to Dublin. A failed priest at fifteen. I began a series of jobs at which I proved a dismal failure. Some of these included plumber's apprentice, bicycle shop assistant, bathrobe fittings assistant and, for a nightmarish week, morgue attendant at St James' Hospital. All in the space of a few months. I returned to school also for a few months. It was a time of what has come to be known in modern parlance as finding oneself. The problem was I didn't even know I was lost.

Slingbacks, Files
and Wet Pavements

In 1965, having had my ears thickened too many times by
teachers who told me I'd be good for nothing bar a pick and
shovel, I told my mother I was leaving school.

'And do you mind telling me what class of job you'll get with
no Inter or Primary?' she asked.

Then one day I showed her this:

> Insurance Brokers, City Centre, require Messenger 15-16. Must
> be willing to work hard. Opportunity for Advancement. Wages
> £3.00 per week.

Mr Horan, the manager, interviewed me. 'There won't be
anything arjous,' he said, sucking a bull's eye. He looked at me
over the top of his glasses. Everything he said sounded like a
threat.

The next day, I signed on and began my first job. It was to last
eighteen months and during that time I learned nothing about
insurance, although I did get a raise of ten shillings but, most
importantly, I fell dangerously in love for the first time since
leaving the seminary.

My duties were simple. Every morning I collected letters
from the various departments, put them in my canvas sack, and
delivered them to the big insurance companies around the city.
This usually took about two hours, allowing half an hour for
gostering and slingeing. Then back to the office to collect the
orders for tea break. Marietta, Ginger Nuts, cigarettes, apple

slices and the like.

My immediate boss was Mr Cuddy and for the rest of the day I worked with him sorting and filing in a dark and dusty room at the top of the building from where you could see out across the grey roofs and chimneys of the city. Mr Cuddy was sixty-four and he was due to retire soon, having worked for the firm for thirty years. Nobody knew as much about files and post as he did, but I think he resented me as an outsider, an intruder. So we lived in uneasy toleration of each other. He was as thin as a pencil and he used to walk to work every day from Rathfarnham with his briefcase and newspaper under his oxter as if he owned the place instead of just working there. In his briefcase he carried sandwiches, a baby Power bottle of milk stopped with brown paper, and a banana. There was always fluff in the fold-ups of his trousers and he wore a green sports coat from Burton's with a pioneer pin which was said to light up in the dark. His hands were long and white with thick blue veins.

At five-thirty every evening during our uneasy truces he would heave the heavy postal franking machine onto the table with a grunt and say, 'They're off'. This was a racing term which he used at all kinds of inappropriate times, because he liked saying it. After he had placed his false teeth on the window sill, we began the endless task of folding renewal notices to fit the windows of the long brown envelopes, before we closed them with our spit. We were always the last to leave, spitless and silent from our file-filled room.

Boredom was broken only by the thoughts of Valerie. The first time I became aware of her she was standing on a ladder in the filing room. She was dressed in a kilted mini skirt with a silver pin at the side. She was eighteen with red hair and green eyes like the sea and she wore fishnet stockings and high sling-back shoes. She worked in typing and she had a boyfriend who worked in Life on the second floor. He played hurling for a team in Finglas. His name was Mícheál. One day I saw them in Henry Street looking in the windows of the shops. She wasn't smiling, just looking from her as if she didn't want to be there at all.

I asked Fanning, who was supposed to be the hard man in relation to women, was she serious about Mícheál. He said he didn't think she was serious about anyone, but she was a great hoult as he himself knew because didn't he have her one night after a do in the Moira. Then sniggering behind his hand he said, 'Fancy a go of her, do you? I'd be careful if I were you. You don't want Mícheál making a *sliotar* out of your little *ceann*.'

Once a week I had to collect all the post from the typing pool and bring it to Mr Horan for signing. This was my opportunity to be near her, to silently adore. Her desk was in front of the window and I watched as in the late afternoons the light traced shadows of her lashes across her cheeks, and her knees whitened against the black net of her stockings! Sometimes wispy tendrils of hair fell about the curves of her neck, and how I longed to know the mystery beneath her blouse as I stood worshipful beside her desk, and she sat provocatively unaware of my messenger boy's presence as her pearl-tipped fingers sped across the keys.

I asked her out the day before Mr Cuddy retired. The firm had a do. All the bigwigs were there. The managing director gave a speech and said it was the end of an era. He was a small thin man, who kept jangling keys and change in his pocket and sniffed the air as if looking for germs. Mr Cuddy made a speech in his telephone voice which nobody could hear but we all clapped and cheered like mad. Then everybody dived on the booze and the little triangular sandwiches.

In the corner Mr Cuddy stood surrounded by everybody, holding his clock and an envelope and looking as if he had just had a fright. His Adam's apple was going up and down in his throat as if it was being pulled by an invisible string. I could see her near the door, standing with Mícheál. He was putting a little sausage on a stick into her mouth and she was laughing. But I knew that tonight as soon as Mícheál got a few pints in him I was going to ask her. And I did. She smiled yes.

Of course I arrived at McBirney's twenty minutes too early. As I lit a Gold Flake and looked in the windows I remembered that my father in his soldier's uniform had met my mother at this exact spot on their first date on a night long gone by.

The rain was falling slantwise under the street light. On the bridge a blind man played 'Come Down the Mountains, Katie Daley' on the accordion, his shirt open. It was bitterly cold and an east wind tore up the dark river and along the quays. I cursed myself for not wearing an overcoat, trying to be the big fellow.

McBirney's clock said twenty past eight. 'Stood up. Stood bloody well up!'

Suddenly, she was behind me. Breathless. Her coat open from running.

'Sorry!' she gasped. 'Couldn't get a bus. Were you waiting long?'

'Nah.' I threw away my fag end. 'Nah, just got here.'

'Oh good,' she said, and took my arm as we heads down, heaved our way against the wind up O'Connell Street towards the Savoy.

The picture was *What a Way to Go*, with Shirley McClaine, my movie girlfriend, and Robert Mitchum. There was a queue. We stamped our feet to keep warm. I offered her a cigarette, striking a match for her. She closed her fingers around mine. Our eyes met. Oh God, her beautiful green eyes. I remembered a poem something about 'Your eyes, they were green and grey, like an April day.' I could think of nothing to say to her — all the great phrases I had rehearsed, cool as you like, in front of the mirror. Instead here I was gabbing about the weather and wishing to God I had stayed at home.

In fearful and awkward ecstasy I watched the screen. I hooked my arm about her shoulders and she laid her head against me. I smelled the strange perfume of her hair. Oh how I longed to kiss her, but fear kept me staring stupidly ahead, my arm paralysed with pain.

And all too soon it was over. We were filing downstairs with the other couples who seemed so at ease with each other out into the cold wet night.

In the pub I spent nearly ten minutes trying to catch the barman's eye, hoping he wouldn't ask me what age I was. As she sipped her brandy, I saw her legs cross and uncross and wondered what the feel of them would be like. Her lips were moving but I didn't know what she was saying, I could only think of my mouth pressed against them. We spent most of the time talking about the office and Mr Horan and she told me that he had chased her around the table after a meeting and begged her to go up the mountains for a drive with him but she said no because he was married. She said he was a right oul' eejit so he was. I wondered would she talk about me the same way, about how I hadn't kissed her once in the pictures and that I hadn't a word to say for myself. I asked her about Mícheál. She smiled as if there were a lot of things she didn't want me to know about.

'Oh look,' she said, 'you've got all froth on your lip.' And she stretched her long pearl-tipped typing fingers towards my mouth and said 'You!' and smiled that smile again.

And of course we missed the last 54. We came around the corner just to see it disappearing into D'Olier Street. So off we trudged, shoulders hunched, clinging tightly to each other, glancing behind now and again to see if the ghost bus might come.

Under the trees near the end of the road she stopped.

'Well, here we are. Home, sweet home.' She pointed to the house at the corner. 'Me mother is still up, otherwise I'd bring you in.'

'That's all right, I have to be off anyway.'

There was silence between us. I was thinking that if I didn't make a move now, I'd regret it forever. Just reach over and kiss her. That's all there is to it. She won't mind. Birds expect you to. She'll be disappointed if you don't. She'll think you're an eejit.

Oh God! My heart was moving sideways in my chest with the fear of it.

'Well, I'll be seeing you tomorrow,' I said, looking at my soaking desert boots.

'Unless there's an earthquake,' she smiled.

Then, 'Aren't you going to kiss me goodnight?' she said, her face turned towards me.

'Oh yeah,' I said, as if it was something I had forgotten. 'Of course.' *I felt her lips against my lips,* clinging and soft. Her arm around my neck pulled me to her, her body moved against mine. No sound but our own breathing and the wind in the trees above us. This is it. You are kissing her! She is kissing you. Don't ever forget this. This is what it's like. This is sex, this is love. 'Oh God, I love you,' I heard myself say. And she laughed her secret laugh into the side of my neck, and I wished that the whole office could have seen us.

After a few seconds she drew away. 'Can I see you again?' I said.

'I suppose so, if you like.'

'What about him — Mícheál?'

'Oh him,' she said in a low voice. 'What he doesn't know, won't hurt him. Goodnight and thanks.'

'Adios,' I said, 'be seeing you.'

She gave me a quick kiss and she was gone. Her slingbacks on the quiet pavement. At the gate she turned and waved and blew a kiss.

When I reached home I realised I'd forgotten my key. I had to jump over the wall and through next door's passageway and into our own back garden. I finally got the kitchen window open and was standing in the sink closing it when the light went on and there was my father standing in his pyjamas.

'What time of night do you call this to be coming in at? I thought you were a bloody robber.'

'I forgot my key.'

'Out straveging the roads by the look of you. Well, I hope she was worth it is all I can say.'

I wanted to say, 'Yes, Da, she is, she's beautiful and I love her and tonight I kissed her for the first time and it's the most exciting thing that's ever happened to me in my whole life.' But he was halfway up the stairs winding the clock and muttering.

The next morning I felt so good about being in love that I woke up early, stole my brother's bicycle and bought twenty Gold Flake to celebrate, even though it was only Wednesday. As I cycled along I kept thinking about her and how dull and boring everybody else's life must be.

It was well after nine when I arrived at the office, but I didn't care. I took the stub of a pencil which was tied to the counter and signed the late book nine-fifteen and wrote my name with a flourish as if I was writing an autograph.

'Out on the ran tan were we, last night?' said a voice behind me.

I turned around and who was it but Mícheál.

'I hope you were gentle with her.' He smirked and took the pencil but he didn't notice the red which coloured my face. His eyes were watery and he smelled of stale beer.

My new boss, a retired policeman, wouldn't speak to me on account of being late, he just grunted when I came in and continued foostering with a bunch of files. But I didn't care. I was in love.

But one morning at the beginning of summer, about three weeks after I had been dating her, I arrived at work to find a letter addressed to me, sitting on the franking machine. Since Mr Cuddy retired I was more or less in charge of the post room. I knew it was from her because it was typed and there was no stamp on it. She was getting engaged to Mícheál and she was sorry but she didn't think it would be a good idea to see each other again. That was all I read before I tore the letter into a thousand pieces and let it fall like snow into the street below.

I decided to leave as soon as I could and answered an advertisement for a job in a toy factory. I could not endure seeing her every day. I cursed Mícheál and tried to understand what she saw in him but I began to hate both of them and couldn't wait to be gone from the place.

On my last day I went to wages to collect my cards and bonus and the bloke behind the bars said, 'You're lucky to be getting out of this kip.'

Mr Horan was cut off from the rest of the office by a glass partition behind which you could see him writing or speaking on the phone, his mouth silently moving like a goldfish. I hadn't been in there since the first day I started work.

'Young Sir,' he addressed me loudly and good humouredly. 'What can I do you for?' That was supposed to be a funny line so I pretended to laugh.

'I wanted to talk to you about . . . I want to leave.'

'I see,' he said, carefully folding the paper around a half-eaten Macaroon bar which was on the desk. 'Not like us? Is that it?' he said. His eyebrow raised over his glasses.

I could think of nothing else to say.

'We thought you were coming on quite well. In fact, we had great hopes for you in Claims. But if you are determined to leave us there is nothing we can do, is there?'

His fists were fat and hairless protruding from under his starched white cuffs.

As I looked at him I couldn't help but feel kind of sorry for him. He was a prisoner as well, destined to be locked up in here for the rest of his life, signing his squiggle and sneaking chocolates.

There were too many people to say goodbye to so I just quietly left my canvas sack with my biroed initials on it on the table in the post room. Fanning said, 'You'll do well for yourself I've no doubt. You won't be sorry to be leaving this old place. Drop in and see us now and again and let us know how you are getting on in the world. Where is it you're off to?'

'I'm getting a job in a toy factory, making teddy bears.'

'Oh well,' he said, 'that'll make a nice change. As long as

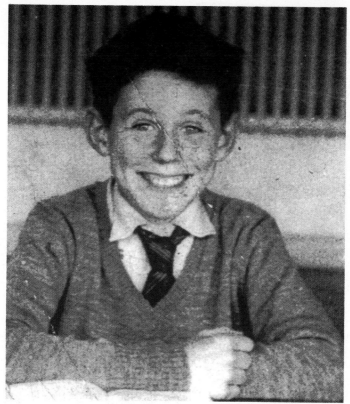

Aged 10 – 'with shining morning face'.

My mother and father on holidays at Lough Key, County Roscommon.

My granny with her friend Mrs Doran
at Rathside.

'My Father'.

With my brother (seated), already two
attempts on his life – a third to come.

The family grows – my sisters Marian and
Breda with me on the left and Tom on the right.

First Holy Communion at Holy Faith Convent, The Coombe. I am second from the right, front row.

Walkinstown 1968. My sisters Marian (left) and Margaret (right) with my mother.

Graduation Day, July 1973. From left: Mary Lennon, Sister Veronica, myself, and my good friend, Mary Healy.

Revisiting the Seminary, 1982.

My first ever role at the Focus Theatre as Dr Kroll in Ibsen's 'Rosmersholm', 1976.

(Photo: Áine O'Connor)

In my teaching days with my Leaving Certificate class on a trip to Spain, 1974.

'White O'Morn' near Kilcolgan, County Galway, which became my Irish home.

1982. To London to seek our fortune: Áine, me and Eddie Dunne's Humber at Carrog, North Wales. (Photo: Sean Lawlor)

I had taken to riding my bicycle through the corridors of the hotel – see 'Movie Minutes'.

At last we reached the village. A strange, silent place with names I would never forget. (Photo: Áine O'Connor)

With Ellen at the White House Washington, 1988.

Hollywood 1994.

you're getting your bag of coal.' And he hit me a blow of farewell to the shoulders and went off guffawing.

Down in the creaking lift to the typing room to look at her for the last time. She was even more beautiful to me than Shirley McClaine, if such a thing were possible, as I watched her sitting beneath the window with the sun a river of light behind her. Once again I realised how much I loved her. The sense of my loss was devastating. But I said no goodbye to her as I left the typing room forever.

—

Some years ago I was walking down the Rathmines Road when suddenly I saw her coming towards me. It was sixteen years since I'd seen her, yet I knew her instantly. She was wheeling a pram and beside her a bearded man was speaking and as she listened, she was smiling. I wondered what had happened to Mícheál. As we passed she flicked her eyes in my direction for a small second only, but not a flicker of recognition crossed her still beautiful face.

My education was interrupted in 1969 when I secured a place at University College Dublin. The experience felt like being trapped in an airport waiting for a flight that kept being delayed. I hated the soulless architecture of the place, the relentless emphasis on exams. I took to wearing a long black policeman's coat, debuttoned of course, given to me by a recently promoted Special Branch man.

I began to write at this time, and had my first story 'A Memory of Daffodils' read on Liam Nolan's programme Here and Now by the actor Chris Curran. With friends we gathered in a pub in Ballybrack and listened. Afterwards I sauntered half-cut through Dun Laoghaire as if I'd lost my virginity but nobody seemed to notice that either. Ah well.

During this time I founded and edited a literary magazine entitled The Bridge and wrote therein under several assumed names. Otherwise Ulick O'Connor, Mary Lavin, John B. Keane, Michael Hartnett, Máirtín Ó Direáin, Christy Brown, Ronan Sheehan and Richard Kearney and the one and only Lee Dunne all gave me pieces which we sold to drunk people in pubs after ten o'clock on weekend nights.

To support myself I took a job as a postman during the Christmas holidays. This next chapter is an account of a paynight after one such turn of duty at Crumlin post office. It was typical of many excursions to town for the craic on Saturday nights. Images and impressions recalled in hangover the following day.

Saturday Night
and Sunday Morning

C hristmas Eve. Cigarette smoke fogs the snug of Mooney's, Crumlin. Tidal rise and fall of song and laughter. Postmen sink pints and slag us, their sissy student helpers of ten days past. 'Another Christmas over. Thanks be to James's Street.'

Army-coated amateurs, we braved the dogs of Walkinstown as we humped our sacks to the sleeping houses. Seeing dark of night turn to grey of morning under the lights of the Ballymount Road.

'Give us a song.'

'I will in me —'

'Her eyes they shone like diamonds.'

'Fair play to you, sunshine.'

'See yez next year, lads.'

'Not if we can help it.'

Swell of laughter.

Every year Aunty K sends a turkey from Kildare. It's hanging now from our kitchen wall. The beak scrapes against my hand. I shiver. A paper star turns the hallway red.

We meet at the roundabout. Joe, Pat, Dave and me. Trousers creased into offensive weapons, smelling of Christmas present Brut, we lounge across the seats of the 77 like gunslingers.

'Fares, please.'

'Dame Street. Keep the change. It's Christmas.'

Twelve chin Doberman conductor with Santa Claus cheeks.

'The git up of youse! I hope it keeps fine for youse! Feet offa dem seats. Bowsies!'

'He's going to burst me one of these days, the size of him,' says Joe.

Urging and cursing the bus around corners, through lights, past queues. A lifetime before the terminus. Skip before the stop. Onto the pavement. Neat as a bird landing on a branch. Oh Dublin is alive and sinning tonight, boys.

Outside Trinity, unseeing, uncaring, a couple are wearing.

'She's ating yer man,' says Dave enviously.

Greenbacks in our pockets courtesy of the P & T.

'Now lads, the crawl is yer only man. From Guiney's to the Half Way House.'

'Ah, I don't agree with this oul' Christmas lark at all at all. Gone too commercial for my liking, so it is.' A mournful night telephonist on his break.

'That's the man that punched Ulick, ye know. Oh yes.'

Dave is saying to a girl. 'And what's Santy bringing *you* for Christmas?'

We leave him and head up the carol singing street. The clink of a collection box. 'Herdlepress.' The smell from Bewleys. The swollen-ankled women laden with parcels. The laughing, linking girls. 'Get the last of the cheeky Charlies.'

'Herdlepress.' It's Barney, shell shocked in a submarine in Kimmage in World War Two, making an art of selling paper.

'Merry Christmas, Barney.'

'Same to you, lads, with knobs on.'

A tinker blows a tin whistle. His sister shakes a cardboard box full of holy pictures. Above the neon pulse of Christmas lights, the sky is riddled with stars. Like spilled drink, the people pour onto the pavements from the roaring pubs. Children look through windows for Das not coming home.

Into the Bailey.

'Hoi. Hawz it goeen?' Aideen from Dalkey, a pint in her hand. 'Loike the malebowt in here. Isntit? Hay. Haven't seen you at lectures for aeons.'

'He was on the hop,' said Pat.

'Ooh I see.'

In the corner a girl cries quietly. Her boyfriend stares ahead, unrepentant.

Outside, girls from a factory with nylon smocks and paper hats push through the crowds.

'Wait for us, Bernie. Me cups is rattlin'.'

At McDaid's a crowd. Two men circle each other like cocks. 'Not so bleedin' tough, now are ye?'

'Stick one on him, Lar.' A voice from the crowd.

'Ah now, come on, lads, break it up, it's Christmas,' someone else calls.

'You shut your mouth.'

The fighters pay no attention. Fierce in their war of stares. So many pubs. So many pints. So few Christmases. Only Joe and me left now. Half past eleven. A snake of a queue outside the chipper, melancholy from celebration.

'Give us two large cod and chips, please.'

'I only got two hands for Christ's sake.'

Sweating Mario. Face like a greyhound, cigarette hanging from his lips. Dreaming of Sorrento in the middle of Dublin.

'Where'll we be this time next year? Or will we be here at all? That's what I want to know,' says Joe.

On the drunken, homeward-heading bus, a man is singing, 'I'm dreaming of a white Christmas.' He thinks he's Bing Crosby, Joe says, but everybody listens. And when he finishes, we all clap and stamp our feet and shout. 'Give us another one, Bing.'

Through the fogged-up windows, the lights of houses pass quickly as all the other Christmases of our lives. The man starts to sing 'Adeste Fideles' but he winds down like a gramophone, not remembering the words.

Someone else starts 'You made me love you. I didn't want to do it.' We all join in, swaying from side to side polishing imaginary windows like Sonny Knowles.

Then the silence of Christmas Eve, the roundabout again. 'Happy Christmas, Joe. See you tomorrow.' A good bit away, I hear them singing in the church — midnight Mass. A bell tolls.

The clock ticks in our hallway. The light from the dying fire flickers on the walls. A car passes. Stillness again. Soon the room is dark except for the candles burning in the window. I am tired. I lean my head against the cool pane. Soon it will be Christmas morning.

For the actor, acting is an addiction that can never be cured. We return to it endlessly, compulsively, like addicts craving a fix; it sets the blood racing wildly and transports us to a world that is of this one, yet is not. We find no release from its cruel illogical demands, yet we embrace it without question again and again whether it brings us joy or not, for there is always the belief, buried deep, that we unlock the doors with a golden key to a time and a place that is beyond dreams, beyond imagination, somewhere between the shadow and the substance.

Hadn't We the Gaiety!

Besides the picture houses of the town, I was drawn inevitably to the theatres. Some of them overwhelmed me, made me feel inferior, as if I had no right to be there. An upstart from Walkinstown. At any moment, a stern-faced usher might come and ask me what my business was and escort me shamefaced to the doors.

My heart always beat faster as I climbed the carpeted steps of the Gate. MacLiammóir, Edwards, Orson Welles, James Mason and other luminaries glaring at me from photographs with undreamt of elegance and haughty inaccessibility.

I mingled, drinking minuscule cups of muddy coffee, listening to the badinage of fur-coated ladies from places like Foxrock. Their escorts always spoke with Trinity or UCD accents and carried boxes of After Eights for them.

'You can't beat a good Shaw, that's what I say.'

'Oh, now Ibsen's my cup of tea.'

'Very mournful, all that Scandinavian doom and gloom with people jumping into mill races and that kind of carry on.'

'Not many laughs I'll grant you but he's the business all the same, Ibsen.'

The Gate was part of the Rotunda Hospital where I was born so it had a special place in my affections. I saw MacLiammóir there playing a French lover in a farce at sixty-two years of age. I heard somebody say at the interval that he was bet into a corset and that he was barely able to breathe, but I was fascinated by him. Why couldn't a lover be sixty-two anyway, I thought. I was there to hear his world-famous one-man show on the life of Oscar Wilde. The pink carnation, the pale pointed hand, the quivering melodrama of that great voice. People said he believed he was the spirit of Wilde reincarnated. The audience made one person by his magic.

Afterwards I would stand outside and look at the photographs of the actors, studying how they stood, the way the camera caught the drama of a passing moment forever, then I would cycle back to Walkinstown repeating lines from the play and trying to imitate the actors.

Of course I would fall in love with every one of the actresses and would follow them from theatre to theatre in different plays. Maureen Toal, Maura Hastings, Patricia Martin, Dearbhall Molloy, Clare Mullen, they became my wish fulfilled Gretas and Marlenes and Marilyns under the lights that turned their skin alabaster and ivory and their eyes to shining jewels. And I would think of myself walking out from stage doors with them, throwing away epigrams like Oscar and looking like Paddy Bedford, my cigarette in a holder, their laughter tinkling in the night like music. I saw Gloria Graham at the Olympia and Broderick Crawford at the Gaiety and Richard Harris and the unknown Pavarotti and Peter O'Toole. And once an Indian actor playing Lord Alfred Douglas the aristocratic lover of Oscar Wilde in a bad blond wig.

'Sure your man's as black as your boot. Bowsie wasn't a black man, he was the son of the Marquis of Queensbury, wasn't he.'

'Sure who cares, he's a very good actor, look at him crying, you can really see him acting.'

I liked the Eblana situated under the CIE bus terminal at Store Street, where the odours of the public convenience wafted through the theatre. I attended an obscure German play there once. Hardly anybody in the audience apart from the first three rows. The piece was more or less a one-hander and the actor was forced to carry two and a half hours of speeches by himself. The curtain parted, the lights dimmed, the actor sat in profile on a bare stage. A whispered voice from the front row, 'Oh Jasus, not him, I can't stand this fella.'

Poor, poor actor, strutting and fretting up on the stage hearing the voice that every actor fears in his heart of hearts.

So I divided my solitary nights crossing the lines between fantasy and reality, moving from picture-house to theatre as the mood took me, feeling alone but part of a crowd, enchanted and seduced by shadows, in love with unattainable actresses and imitating my favourite actors. I could never have believed that one day I would appear on these very stages and come to know these people I had worshipped from afar and be proud to call them colleagues, and in some cases dear, dear friends.

But first I had to serve my time, to learn the ropes, hone my craft, as they say. And so I joined an amateur drama group.

I found myself walking nervously up a street of dreary old houses in the south part of the city, 'til I came to an address I had been given. I was admitted to a room full of actors, and most importantly, for this was the real reason I had come, actresses.

There were bank girls and shop girls in tight jeans and they were laughing and at ease with each other. I was introduced to them all and wondered which of them I might have a chance of getting off with. I put my eye on a large-breasted girl from Limerick who was obviously the leading lady. She had a habit of tossing her hair back from her face and stamping her foot. She reminded me of a race horse.

The auditions were soon in progress. An elderly man who sounded like a radio news reader was the obvious star. Everyone looked at him with deference and respect when he spoke. He had been an amateur actor for over thirty years. 'Played all the great roles you know, oh yes, I played Lear at twenty-three.'

'That was some achievement,' I tell him.

'Oh yes I got great crits for that and there are still some people who say I should have taken the gold at Athlone that year.'

'What was your favourite role?'

'Oh, God, now you have me, where do I begin? Well, obviously the old bard, he knew his stuff, old Shakespeare. We did a remarkable modern-dress Hamlet — ground-breaking really.'

'Were you Hamlet?' I asked.

'Indeed I was,' he answered averting his eyes modestly. He beamed upon me, warming to me. 'Have you much experience yourself?'

'No, none at all, actually.'

'Well that's no matter, just keep your eyes open, learn what you can. Very important to have good diction you know, pronunciation so that they understand you, and of course projection so that they can hear you. You must learn to breathe from here, the diaphragm.'

He draws in his stomach and his chest swells out so that for some reason he reminds me of a large wardrobe. He booms out, 'So shaken as we are, so wan with care, Find we have time for frighted peace to pant ...'

Several of the girls are startled and put their hands to their chests and then smile when they realise what's going on.

'Do you see,' he says, 'that's what you need — resonance. Put your hand there, on my chest. Do you feel the vibration?'

I take my hand away and I try to get over to the girl from Limerick. 'I saw Larry's Moor, oh my God, now that was acting.'

'Who's Larry Moore?' I asked him.

'Olivier, Lawrence Olivier,' he snaps. 'Met him once, you know, oh yes. Did I ever tell you about the time I met Orson?'

I drift away but he calls me back. At last I am delivered when the director claps his hands for silence. We are each to read a piece from the play and based upon that reading we will be cast. I am to play the part of grandfather in two small scenes in a schools production.

I made an undistinguished debut in a cold room in Malahide. I took part in a series of amateur productions over the next couple of years, the highlight of which was playing Guildenstern, opposite Myles Dungan in Tom Stoppard's play, *Rosencrantz and Guildenstern are dead.*

We reached the final of the south Leinster drama festival at Gorey, where I won an award for my playing, though the adjudicator, Betty Anne Norton, in her summation criticised me for my diction and then advised me to learn how to breathe properly from the diaphragm. I still have that plaque, although the leg fell off it in a melée after the first night party. There are those who would still say that Betty Anne was correct.

I continued to teach as a relief teacher in vocational schools all over Dublin, finally coming back to my old Alma Mater, Ard Scoil Éanna on the Crumlin Road.

It was during this time that I met a flame haired female Hamlet called Deirdre O'Connell who ran the Focus Theatre, a tiny garage off the Pembroke Road. She was a well known figure about the streets of the city, dressing in customary suits of solemn black as she rushed about putting up posters for plays, or begging money from the Arts Council to keep her tiny theatre alive. Instantly I fell in love with her selfless dedication, her integrity and singleminded pursuit of excellence. She was a brilliant actress steeped in the Stanislavski method and had taught some of the country's best actors, like Tom Hickey and Johnny Murphy and Tim McDonnell. Her gentle demeanour belied her extraordinary energy and her commitment to giving Dublin alternative classical theatre. We met in a restaurant of check table-cloths just off Pembroke Road and she asked me to join the company to do Ibsen's *Rosmersholm.*

I entered for the first time the world of real theatre in that tiny, cold, unheated, musty smelling space. Anything I ever learned about acting this woman taught me. If the Irish theatre has a heroine it is she, who taught me that passion and commitment and love of the work were more important than any technique. My tenure at the Focus was one of the happiest times of my life as an actor. My salary of two pounds a week was, I felt, an undeserved bonus and I left my teaching job every evening with a sense of profound exhilaration.

One summer's morning I was called from my class to take a telephone call from Peter Sheridan, who was then with his brother Jim the artistic brilliance behind the emerging Project Theatre. I agreed to join the fledgeling company and from that day on I knew my life as a teacher was coming to an end. The Project became, under the direction of the Sheridan brothers, the most exciting venue of the arts to emerge from Dublin since the days of The Pike. It had sprung up as an inevitable alternative to the staid predictability of the more established theatres. Jim Sheridan proved to be a stunningly innovative and original whirlwind that swept through the mediocrity of Dublin theatrical life. An acting style developed, rooted in naturalism, heavily influenced by Sheridan's Brechtian tendencies that soon became the most exciting in the city. Talented actors began to emerge, like Garreth Keogh, Mannix Flynn, Paul Bennett, Peter Caffrey, Olwyn Fouere, Liam Neeson, Noel O'Donovan, Frank Melia, Vincent McCabe, Gerald McSorley, Susan Slott, Colm Meaney, Johnny Murphy and Sir Alan Stanford among others. It became known as a theatre of excitement and originality, where risks were taken and convention was defied. Now and then we were joined by other established players like Godfrey Quigley, Kevin Flood, the wonderful Tom Irwin, Maureen Toal and Paddy Long.

It was here too that Neil Jordan, our most original and innovative film-maker, began his career.

We all felt part of something special that was happening because of the unique combination of chemistry and circumstance and it was here that we premiered the ground-breaking production of *The Liberty Suit*, which was to be my professional debut. The prison life of Mannix Flynn, written by himself in collaboration with Peter Sheridan and directed by Jim Sheridan received rave reviews and standing ovations when it transferred to the Olympia Theatre in October 1977. The Project had arrived. It was in a way the beginning of an artistic explosion that gave rise to a great deal of what has happened in theatre and film in Ireland over the last twenty years.

—

Finally the day comes. I will leave teaching forever. I feel sadness, excitement too. Summer sun floods the staff-room. My colleagues sit about at break-time, sipping tea with crumbling Marietta. Fingers stained with ink, gowns with chalk. How they all long for summer and freedom, far flung Mullingar and Morocco.

'You can always come back,' somebody says, 'if it doesn't work out — the acting.'

This reassures me. I will miss the sound of bells to circumscribe my days, the playground squeals.

Yet I know in my soul I should go. I have never been a great teacher. No Mr Chips as I fondly hoped. I am barely older than my pupils, and they do not believe my authority, but I have tried to give, to nurture, to plant flowers in their souls.

The children chase each other across the yard, the smokers sneaking to the toilets. Mr Brosnan stands before the window, a stick behind his back, rarely used. White-haired, pound notes, pipes, biros in the top pocket of his Clery's coat. Fluent Greek, Latin. A lover of words and philosophy and poetry. Now my colleague, he used to be my teacher. My admiration for him is great. 'You would have been happy,' I tell him, 'sitting beneath the tree with Aristotle.'

'Yes,' he smiled, 'I would.'

'I hope you'll be happy,' he says.

'I hope so too.'

'Think of us now and then.'

'I will.'

'Are you afraid?' he asks unexpectedly.

'Of what?' I ask.

'Of leaving.'

'Yes. But more scared that I'll have to come back.'

'There is nothing to fear,' he says, 'except the one thing.'

'What is that?' I ask.

'You will find it,' he smiles.

In the assembly they are all gathered about. The head mistress is making a speech about me. I have been a student here and later teacher. I am an example, she says. They will be sorry to lose me, but I am following my star. 'Maybe one day we'll see him at the Abbey.'

'The Abbey bar,' the science teacher whispers to me and laughs.

As a token of esteem for four years amongst them, she presents a silver goblet. May the road rise with me, it says in Gaelic. There is loud clapping, cat calls are shushed.

The air heavy with sadness and silence, I stumble through my thanks, realising that I do not want to leave now. To face the uncertain future. To lose my A post. To risk failure. To lose my friends, my students, my routine, my respect and security, all for the sake of a play at The Project in which I speak twelve lines.

In the pub afterwards. Pints of Smithwicks. Cheese and crackers.

'Let me tell you something,' one of the teachers says. 'You are making the biggest mistake of your life, but that's just my opinion.'

'You think so?'

'Just think about it.'

'I have.'

'Well then?'

'I believe I'm making the right decision.'

'We'll see, but that's just my opinion. I hope you don't mind. I'm just saying what I think.'

'Not at all.' I am plunged into despair.

Werburgh Street Labour Exchange. A sullen girl from the country demands my name and details without looking at me.

'Sign here,' she says and turns to talk in a soft friendly voice to her colleagues. I take the stub of the pencil that is tied by twine to the counter and smudge my name across the paper. She takes it back without looking at me and orders me to wait on a long seat with the other men.

'Are you afraid somebody will steal your pencils?'

She does not answer.

The notes are crisp, new. Dole money. I'm on the rock 'n'roll, the Labour. Getting the few shillings. I'm an actor, an artist. I swagger with a sense of new born identity. Artist, me bollocks. The only thing you can draw is the dole.

The new man. Take a look at me. Gone the cavalry twills, the tweed jacket, the check shirt, the brown brogues. Look at me now, boys, the strolling player, the thespian, the actor laddie.

Every theatre has its pub where actors come to be themselves — the Abbey, the Flowing Tide — the Gate, the Viscount. But my favourite was always Sinnott's in South King Street, just across from the Gaiety. Sinnott's with its marble counters and snug and old mirrors where actors danced on tables and jumped through windows, poured pints over each other, cashed cheques, got morose, lamented the lack of decent roles and new playwrights, cursed theatrical nepotism and monopoly, debated what theatre should be and what it never is, reminisced about plays they were in and who the best playboy was. They bitched, gossiped, philosophised, learned lines, sang and were shushed, gave coppers to tinkers who raided the snug like lightning, loved each other and fought with each other, talked the hours and years away under a ticking clock, 'til one day the blinds came down for the final time, Joxer, and the darling place was no more. We pass it now and say, pointing to an empty space, 'That's where Sinnott's used to be, used to drink in there in the old days.'

—

'Your man's an actor, be Jasus.'

'Wouldn't ye know by the cut of him. Blue jeans, cowboy boots scuffed, shirt without collar, miner's belt, waistcoat, the face unshaved, the hair uncut. A pint in one hand, a fag in the other. The warm camaraderie of fellow players. The breed apart. The flamboyant, devil may care, tomorrow we die, on the one road, passing this way but once, get up the yard. What do we not give? — A bollicks — That's what we don't give.'

The play is *Dev, the Life and Times of Eamon de Valera*. My part is Arthur Griffith, patriot leader. I wear glasses and a moustache. I feel the spirit of Griffith in me as I speak my twelve lines. I am the living image it seems.

'D'you know who you look like?' another actor says.

'Who?'

'Groucho bleedin' Marx.'

In the reviews I am not mentioned.

Days and nights at the Project. This is my life now. I have rented a room on the South Circular Road. I live on fruit and fish fingers and grilled tomatoes. Still, it's mine. An actor's pad.

Below me, a struggling singer Leonard Cohen O'Reilly, at night keeps me awake, singing his own compositions.

> *'I need inspiration*
> *In all the world I do girl*
> *I love you down the line*
> *Cause we're just spasms of time.'*

'Shut up, for Jazes' sake!'

One night I forget my key. Kick the door into the room. I don't bother to repair it.

'I wouldn't say it's a kip, your flat, but it's the only place in Dublin you have to wipe your feet on the way out.'

Rowdely-dows, come-all-yes that end with the dawn. Groupies, hash, grass and pints, Timmons', The Long Hall, Sinnott's, The Flowing Tide. Pushing in doors, script under arms, rehearsals over, the actors are here, make way. The usual, lads?

'Jasus, I needed that.'

'It's comin' on, act two is. Still a bit slow though.'

'A teacher?'

'Yeh, I used to be, hard to believe I know, but there ya have it. Same again, Danny.'

I have a girl now, tall and beautiful. We are inseparable. We take a flat together on the Pembroke Road. Áine O'Connor of RTE and myself. Love and pain and the whole damn thing.

My father sits in the lounge of The Cherry Tree, with his friend Jimmy. Their days spent at Mass, the pub and the horses.

'I hear he's joined a circus. Gave up the dry leg job? Well, fair play to him. I'd say bein' in a circus is no joke. Ya have to be cut out for that caper. Tell us, would he make e're a few bob at it?'

I am appearing at the National Stadium in a show called *The Point*. Set in the land of Point where everything has a point — except this production, I quickly come to realise. I have replaced Shay Healy in the role of the rock man in which I am encased in a rubber rock and mime to a pre-recorded track. I am a poor dancer. Áine, my girl, spends Christmas night teaching me steps and on St Stephen's Day we open. The show is not good, technically or otherwise. Attendances fall off rapidly. Free tickets are distributed to ungrateful audiences who eat crisps and shout abuse at us. One day as we bow, I hear a man in the front row proclaim, 'Give it up, for Jasus' sake, yis are useless.' Wind whips around the auditorium from the South Circular.

Suddenly the gorgeous Alma Carroll is forced by a fault in the sound system to sing the same line over again. Only the eyes betray her panic.

John Le Mesurier from *Dad's Army* and Mark Lester, from the adorable movie *Oliver*, seem bewildered.

My brother comes to see the show and says, 'Jasus, that was crap. I don't know how yez do it. By the way, you'll have to get those varicose veins looked after.'

'What varicose veins?' I ask. I am standing in a pointed hat and purple tights.

'There.' He points to my ankles where two ridges are visible. 'The least you could do,' he says, 'is take off your bleedin' socks.'

I am called to RTE and secure a part in a play called *The Last of Summer* by Kate O'Brien. I read through the script looking for my part and finally, there it is. My first role in front of a camera. A priest who shows Susan Fitzgerald through a door. I am disappointed to realise that my dialogue consists of 'This way, please.' Still, it's a break, of sorts.

'Better actors than you had more infelicitous beginnings,' my friend and now my acting mentor Christy says. 'Give it the lash.'

'How can I give "This way, please" the lash?'

'A great actor can steal the show with no lines.'

'I don't want to steal a show. I just want to be there a bit more.'

'Anyway, what does your character feel? That's what's important.'

'He agrees with me.'

At home, I experiment. I have called my character Father O'Connor. He comes from Kildare I have decided. 'Dis weh, please,' I intone in priestly fashion. But the Kildare accent doesn't really go. I give him a smile. It seems cheeky and flirtatious. I am shy, do not raise my eyes and make him from the north. A shy northern priest. I have it.

I try it out for Christy. 'This way, please.'

'Mmm,' he muses. 'Say it again.'

I oblige.

'Mmm,' he says again. 'There's somethin' missing. Give 'im a limp.'

'A limp — for what?'

'A childhood accident. Became reclusive, religious.'

I reluctantly limp to the table. 'This way, please.'

'You have it. That's it. I can feel the pain of the man. He's flesh and blood.'

'You think so?'

'Trust me,' says Christy.

In the rehearsal room it finally comes to my scene. I limp towards the door, with a frozen smile for Susan Fitzgerald who is beautiful and poised. By now I have relocated Father O'Connor's birthplace to Ballymena.

'This way, please.' I open the door, close it behind her and turn to face the applause of the astonished cast and crew. What a performance! What reality. What subtext. What depth.

The director calls me aside, obviously not wishing to upset the others by allowing them to overhear the compliments he will heap upon me. 'Is there something wrong with your foot?' he asks.

'Why?' I ask.

'You're limping badly there. I just noticed it.'

'No. That's Father O'Connor's limp.'

'Who's Father O'Connor?'

'I mean my character — Father O'Connor is what I call him.'

'I see.'

'I'm in character.'

'You are? That's all right. I just thought there — there was something wrong with your foot. But listen, forget the limp. It doesn't work. It's distracting. And by the way, was that a Cavan accent you were using there?'

'No, actually it was Ballymena.'

'I see. Listen, just forget the accent. Your own accent is grand.'

'Anything else?'

'Just throw away the line. "This way, please" — you see?'

I repeat 'This way, please.'

'There you are. You seem to be threatening poor Susan. I think you gave her a bit of a start.'

My priest's collar is too big. I feel like I am looking out of a basin. I have developed an allergy rash from my costume. I have to walk in a mincing, affected manner. The director calls out, 'You're not a hairdresser.'

Filming day. I am nervous. Repeating my line over and over till it makes no sense and sounds like Hungarian.

All is set for my scene. Technicians, make-up, cameras, lights. It could be Hollywood. Action. Silence. I open the door. I am overtaken by the moment and am excited into an impromptu move which brings me further into the room than is rehearsed. This is called danger in acting, I think to myself. I remain there smiling, priestly. The silence is electric. Those moments of magic on stage rarely, if ever, experienced even by the most gifted.

'That will be all, Father. Please close the door on your way out,' says Barry Cassin who plays the bishop. He says the word 'out' with such force — a snarl almost — that my actor's instinct warns me that he may have been excited into overacting. Unexpected for such an actor.

I turn and smash into a huge statue of the Blessed Virgin which in slow motion topples and breaks in a thousand pieces on the concrete floor. I sink slowly to the ground as if in a dream. People are running towards the statue with frozen horror on their faces. I lie there as they pick up the pieces of plaster and glare at me.

'The nuns'll kill us. They lent it to us. We'll never get this repaired.' The man is almost crying. 'Why didn't you stick to the moves you rehearsed, ya eejit?'

'My character moved. It just felt right ... for him.'

'Don't be trying to blame this on anyone else.'

'Anyway, apart from all that,' I stumble, 'how was the scene?'

—

Once I saw Mícheál MacLiammóir. A hero. An evening in summer by the canal where the water roars Niagarously onwards. A yellow cravat at his throat, a Crombie coat, an ivory cane.

Now almost blind. I salute him because I think I may never have the opportunity again.

'Dia dhuit,' I say.

'Dia 's Muire dhuit.'

That was all. Just a greeting. A frail old man, tiny steps like a child as he moved toward Harcourt Street. But as is the way of such meetings, I knew that I as a stranger had passed from his life, but I would remember him forever. People cried when he died. Cried for what had been, for the joy he brought into their lives. The doors of magic and wonder he opened. They were sorry they would never see his like again. They said he could have gone to Hollywood, but chose instead to remain in Dublin. I keep the memory of that evening like a faded photograph in a drawer.

—

I am cast in a production of *The Marat Sade*, a play about the divine Marquis. My friend, Paul Bennet, spends the evening covered in plastic boils, declaiming from a tin bath-tub and being abused by Sir Alan Stanford who parades about the stage bedecked in lace and tight trousers. The rest of us are fittingly cast as lunatics of various hues. The stage is enclosed and we cannot remove ourselves, even at the interval. Because this is an avant garde play, we must make like we really are inmates, whilst the audience move among us drinking tea and desperately trying to ignore us.

'What do you think?' a man from Ballsbridge says.

'Very . . . theatrical,' says his wife. 'Pity they wouldn't stick to something more . . . mmm . . . accessible.'

Mannix Flynn who wears a white hospital gown and a pointed pixie hat bounces between them and whispers, 'I'm gettin' out tomorrow.'

'Well, that's good. Where?'

'Out of the asylum.'

'That's great news.'

'I have a bad back.'

'Very sorry to hear it,' says the man from Ballsbridge, stirring his tea and looking away.

I play the mad priest, Jacques Roux. I am encased in a strait-jacket and wear a long black wig. I am uncertain of my motivation.

'You're mad. That's your motivation,' the director tells me. 'Just be yourself.'

Now and then I jump up and deliver inordinately long harangues at the audience who are frozen into perplexed catatonia.

Mannix Flynn swings across the stage on a rope screaming 'I'm a mad aminal.'

'It's animal, Mannix — A-N-I-M-A-L — not aminal.'

'Did you know Voltaire? Did you?'

'No.'

'Then shut the fuck up. I am a mad aminal,' he screams again.

All around the stage are extras dressed as asylum attendants. They are under orders to prevent us from escaping to the dressing-rooms. I lumber up to one fierce-looking man who wields a rubber truncheon.

'Let us out for a minute,' I beg.

He is impassive. 'Silence, comrade,' he says.

'Jasus, I just want to have a smoke. Please.'

He delivers a thundering blow with his truncheon to my unprotected head sending my wig skew-ways.

'You have betrayed the revolution and the people of Paris,' he shouts as I stagger away under a battery of blows that bring up clouds of dust from my strait-jacket.

One night I am so bored I fall asleep. On stage. Nobody seems to notice. I wake as my fellow actors are taking their bows.

Rehearsals have encouraged dramatic experiment. 'I want,'

says one actor, 'to have a look of wonder. The lunatic-as-child concept.'

He has sellotaped his eyebrows, giving him a look of comic derangement. 'What do you think?' he asks us.

'Cool for cats, but can you see where you're going?' somebody says.

'That's the whole point,' he explains enigmatically.

Later he concusses himself after blindly running into the back wall. There are times when the process of the actors' preparation escapes me.

—

Once when I was a child walking with my father in the park, we came upon a group of actors performing *The Cat and the Moon* by W.B. Yeats. They are masked and costumed in coarse sacking and they speak to the audience conspiratorially as if it were another character. I am enthralled at these strange creatures from another world who speak such bizarre and lovely words.

At the end of the performance they remove their masks to reveal their earthly faces. So ordinary and yet so unreal that I think for a time they must in turn remove those masks as well. Their eyes shine as they bow. With an inner light it seemed, at once shy, yet full of mysterious and strange power. I never forget that look, and I have seen it thousands of times at curtain calls on stages all over the world.

—

A Sunday in summer 1978. I arrive at the gate in RTE. I am flagged down by the security man. I am here for a screen-test for *The Riordans*.

He is unimpressed. It is a day that will change my life. Because it is Sunday, the building is empty. At once I am attacked by the oul' nerves as I walk the silent corridors to the studio. I am to perform a scene with Biddy White-Lennon. She is known to everybody in Ireland as Maggie, the wife of Benjy Riordan. I will test for a character called Pat Barry. 'The cowboy' (in the sense of 'a roughish fellow' as in 'he's a right cowboy, that fella'). I have surmised that there may be a risqué element to the scenes, Maggie being a married woman and I being a single farm helper. Shades of Lady Chatterley and Mellors. Biddy is somebody I have watched on Sunday nights for years. To me she is one of the Riordans, the most famous family in Ireland. I am appalled to hear myself call her Maggie, but she is kind and courteous to me. She has a welcoming smile. Bored technicians stand about. One of them sits high on a chair with a microphone pole, eating a sandwich.

I have memorised the scene so that I know not just my words, but hers as well. When I hear myself deliver her first line and call her Pat she is nonplussed.

'No, you're Pat,' she says.

'Oh thanks,' I say.

'That's all right. Take your time,' she says.

Before us on the table is a ball of knitting wool. She suggests that I hold this during the scene. It calms me. I think of my rehearsal with my friend Christy.

'Acting for the screen is a different kettle of fish. You don't have to do anything. Well, not nothin'. You have to be doin' somethin', but give the illusion of doin' nothin'. D'ye see?'

'I think so.'

'Give us a look at your mush. Which is your best side?'

'I don't know. Me nose has been broken three times.'

He turns me this way and that. 'Right side, deffo. Now, have ye ever watched John Wayne in action?'

'Of course.'

'And Kirk Douglas and Randolf Scott and Jeff Chandler. What did they all have in common?'

'Cowboys?'

'The jaw,' he says.

'The what?'

'You have to give it the jaw when the camera is on. See? Grind your teeth like so and get a look of "I don't give a bollicks" and you're away on a hack.' And he shows me how to do it. 'It's called sexual insouciance.'

I hold the ball of wool and now I remember Christy's advice. I give it the jaw and get that look and hold it and the director says, 'Give him the line, somebody.'

But Biddy and I connect. There is chemistry between us and the sandwich-eating sound man says 'Pretty good' and Biddy says 'That was great' and I say 'Do you think so?' and she says 'I know so.'

Noel O'Brien is the director. He is patient and encouraging and he makes me do the whole thing again and again and suddenly I begin to feel it and I know I've done it and so does he. I am going to be the cowboy. I am going to be in *The Riordans*.

A few months later as I walk down the Rathmines Road I am stunned by the sight of myself on the cover of the *RTE Guide*. 'The new man in *The Riordans*,' it says. This family of actors welcomes me, but they little realise that I will be a sign that things are about to change. I am uncomfortable with the costume I am given and exchange it for a black coat and a scarf of my own. It seems to fit the character, Pat.

I watch the first episode with my family. My father is thrilled. *The Riordans* and *The Honeymooners* are his favourites. He cannot believe it's me on the screen. Nor can I. He looks to me and then to the screen again. At last he says, 'Isn't television an amazing thing all the same? There you are,' he says pointing at me, 'and there you are,' he says pointing at the cowboy.

Now I am stopped in the street. There are letters from strangers. I am recognised everywhere I go. I am asked for my autograph. One day in the country I come out of a pub and there are crowds of people cheering and applauding in the street. I think there must be something going on. I am shocked when I realise they've come for me. I am mortified and want to run and hide somewhere. This kind of attention makes me uncomfortable. I have always hated being singled out in public. I think of myself as intensely private. Ironic then, I should have chosen this life. Acting is the shy man's revenge, T.P. McKenna told me once in the Horse Show House in Ballsbridge.

Once, a woman drives her car onto the pavement as she turns her head to see if it's me or not. But I am no longer me. I am somebody else I do not recognise and people say things to me that I cannot fathom.

'How're ye, Pat?'

'Begob, you're an awful man.'

'You look much different in real life nor ye do in reality.'

'Sign this.'

'Come here.'

'Can we get a photograph?'

'Here, come 'ere, ya boy ya, are ye slippin' it to Maggie? Wait till Benjy comes home, by Jasus, he'll put manners on you.'

'You look bigger on the screen.'

'Are you who I think you are?'

'Are you yer man?'

'Is it yourself?'

One day the cast are called into a meeting. There is beer, coffee and sandwiches that curl at the sides. The cast are told they are no longer needed. After eighteen years. This is the end. There is silence. People are crying. Others dazed, hands to their mouths, disbelieving in shock like people at the scene of a traffic accident. After eighteen years of constant employment. These actors are their characters now. They have been sucked dry like oranges and thrown away. The future looks bleak. For most of them, the programme has been their lives.

But for me it's another story. I am to star in a new series based on a character Wesley Burrowes has created. My life is to change even more, in ways I never believed possible two short years before. *Bracken* is about to begin — but that's another story.

I lived in London from 1982 to 1986. During this time I worked at the National Theatre, the Royal Court, and began my career in British films starring in Defence of the Realm *and playing Lord Byron in Ken Russell's* Gothic.

Áine and I had left Dublin in a Humber I'd bought for four hundred pounds from Eddie Dunne, a film transport driver, who'd driven everybody from James Cagney to Sean Connery. He showed me a crack in the mahogany dashboard one day. 'See that? You know who done that? James Cagney,' he said proudly. 'In a desperate temper one morning, gave the dashboard an awful clout.' It was a legendary auto, leather seats, a cocktail cabinet in the rear, ivory steering wheel. It served me faithfully for five years. When it got towed away to the scrap it was like losing an old friend.

I began to make some money and we bought a grand house overlooking Hampstead Heath beside Boy George. But often we would venture over to Kilburn and Cricklewood where my best friend Sean Lawlor lived and we drank and sang the songs of our own people and danced sometimes to the visiting Irish showbands for the craic. It was there that I met another Sean, a labourer from Limerick who became my friend.

For my friend Sean of Kilburn

E arly morning. Rain falls in sheets over the grey roofs of Kilburn, Broadway. On the quiet Sunday streets, the occasional walkers bend against the wind that comes down from Hampstead Heath. Underneath the pavements, now and then, the underground thunder of a train. You are standing in a doorway of a locked-up shop-front awaiting opening time. Ill-fitting brown Sunday suit, white shirt open at the collar, the Irish papers under your arm. Feet apart, hands deep in trouser pockets, eyes hunting for momentary contact and I pass, hoping to avoid that look I've caught so often in these streets.

'Mora,' you say.

'Mora,' I reply. And reluctantly I stand with you in the doorway, help you through the pain of waiting for the doors of the King's Arms to let you in.

'East wind,' you nod.

'You'd get your end.'

I have come to know your story, Sean.

I'd watch you drunk, bent over the juke-box, playing and re-playing the 'Rose of Aranmore'. A white mark at the top of your forehead. The skin there protected by the peak of your cap from the building site in all weathers.

In Kilburn you went along to the dance at the Hibernian. And stood with your mates along the wall and waited your moment, and danced, though you felt foolish, and truth to tell, never had much of a way with the women you met there. You told me that once. Seldom you asked one. A nurse from Carlow once, I remember. You went drinking and to the pictures but words would not come to hold her interest, and feeling yourself ignorant and idiotic under this shyness, you let her go, and she left you, without sorrow.

Winter and summer, week after month became one, 'til the years flashed by like telegraph poles past a speeding train. Never moving beyond Kilburn and ill-lit damp rooms. Places to sleep, no more. The countless mornings waiting in the half-light for the ghost bus. Sitting in the caff. A mug of tea. A fry. *The Daily Mirror* and a Player. Waiting for the van to pick you up to take you to the site in your uniform of cap and donkey jacket and dungarees and the never-ending day 'til knock-off and the caff again, and at six to the pub. Irish football talk. 'Do you think the Lilywhites'll ever get out 'a Leinster?' Until the towel over the tap signalled finally another day has ended, and walking back among the shabby streets, mostly alone, you sometimes nodded and smiled at strangers in your countryman's way, not because you knew they would stop to talk, but because it was an instinct in you and made you feel a part of things.

I remember you told me once of the night before you left, kneeling by the table in the kitchen, silent save for the sound of your parents' voices as they recited the rosary for your safe journey under the red flicker of the Sacred Heart lamp. In the early morning you left, closing the gate behind you for the last time, not looking back because you dared not, but knowing they were standing there, framed in the doorway, watching, denying their tears.

And standing on the deck of the mail-boat as Dún Laoghaire disappeared, your sadness became a joy. The joy of being free from them, from the town, and its people, and from Ireland. For you, as long as you can recall, there is the coming and the going, the talk of it and the dream of it. You have left and you have returned, relentlessly, compulsively, all your days. The wild goose, homesick after his own kind, torn between the agony of leaving and the fear of staying. Knowing that to be emigrant

At the Venice Film Festival with Áine in 1985 for the premiere of Costa-Gavras' Hanna K.

Dublin 1985. In Mooney's Pub, Phibsboro, with actors (from left) Noelie O'Donovan, Frank Melia and Paul Bennett. (Photo: Seán Lawlor).

Jack, Ellen and myself, Rome, 1990

Séamus Healy 'called up for us then / his ancient boyhood hills / and fields of Kerry / and a homecoming dawn / in a once upon a time'.

Fatherhood on Fourteenth Street, New York, with Jack, 1990.

'The actor prepares'. Filming in Norway, 1990.

At home in Hampstead, London, 1985.

Getting back to roots with Jack in the garden of
White O'Morn, County Galway.

Filming 'Siesta' in Spain with Ellen Barkin, my future wife. And wearing my First Communion Medal, later stolen there.

Arriving at the New York Premier of 'The Untouchables' with Ellen.

With Richard Burton filming on Lake Geneva, 1982. Out of concern for Burton's privacy, I never asked to have my photograph taken with him – much to my regret now.

Fatherhood!

My mother in Hollywood – in the garden of my house with Brando's house in the background.

My children Jack and Romy, Hollywood 1994.

(Photos: Linda Chen)

On location, 'Into the West', 1992. From left, Jack and Ellen with Rory Conroy and Ciarán Fitzgerald.

My great friend, Seán Lawlor.

Deirdre O'Connell of the Focus Theatre.

With John McDonagh,' Into the West', 1992.

and immigrant and stranger is to be one and the same, and that
you belong to all places and to no place at all.

I have met your like, familiar strangers, a thousand times in
Camden and Coventry and Glasgow, carrying exile like a
hump, seeking solace in drink and wandering talk of home and
sometimes fierce hatred of England. I know at once the plough-
man's walk on city streets, the stand, the cut of you, the way
you hide your fag from the wind, even in a bar, between the
thumb and middle finger.

But there was a Sunday long ago in the land of your dreams,
as you readied for Mass, the sound of your boots on an empty
road, the shortcut through a field of barley, the women waving
from modest bicycles, the mora of friends and neighbours, the
men in Sunday suits, caps at a tilt, the wheezing of the organ,
the parade of girls to communion, and you on one knee kneeling on a handkerchief, watching for the shy, sly glance of the
one true love you never knew. And after, the talk of football and
cattle and women and the price of things, of those who stayed
and those who are gone.

I have listened to your sad songs of home, made sadder by
the drink, the head down, the eyes closed, singing the soul's
pain in the King's Arms on a Friday night, dreaming of the old
bog road and Nancy Allen and a nation once again and the
young men who gave their lives for the cause of liberty high
upon the gallows tree.

I remember one night, drunk and boasting on whiskey, you
opened a map of Ireland, and closing your eyes, brought your
finger down on the county of Galway and told us you were
retiring there when you had made your 'millin pounds'. And
though drunk, swore among the laughter that you would do it,
and often in bars, on building sites, you dreamed of a small
house, thatched, among wet green fields and the smell of cattle
and the sea beyond and a wife to share it with you in the end of
your days, and maybe a child or two.

You never made it back, my friend. Sean. You went out the

way you'd have liked. During a feed of beer on a Friday night in the tap-room of the King's Arms, at the counter you put your head in your arms, a fag still smoking in the ashtray, a pint almost full and you fell asleep. Forever.

Movie Minutes

The train stopped among the trees. A squeal of brakes. Shunting and then quiet. Outside the window, snow dropped silently from the branches of firs. Everything white and still. Then people came into my compartment. In dumb show offering me bread, cheese, wine. Weathered Slavic faces. They watched me with curiosity. Smiling, nodding.

'Kaput, choo-choo?'

They looked at one another and repeated 'choo-choo'. They laughed. At last the train moved. By the time we arrived I was drunk. We had been singing for hours, laughing, pantomiming, sharing the bottles. On the platform, the cold sliced through us. We embraced as old friends. 'Yes, I will come your house,' and 'You must come my hotel.' All talking at once.

Hotel a disappointment. Glass box without atmosphere. Beds, hard, single. Decor dominantly brown with variations on brown. Even at check-in desk, began to feel claustrophobic. Kept telling myself that most hotels can seem like home after a few days, once you get adjusted. At least the rooms look on to the sea, and the mountains beyond. Tomorrow in the light everything would be different. I ordered tea with milk. Half an hour later yoghurt with orange juice arrived. I was so tired, yet I knew I would not sleep. I was worried about this film. Also I was worried about M who does not seem to be getting better at all. They are trying to make out it's not progressive, but we know it's only a matter of time.

February 6th

A meeting to discuss script. All of the cast, British and American have arrived except A, our star. He is due tomorrow. Has a reputation for being 'troublesome', i.e. perhaps he doesn't let studios or producers walk all over him.

We all gather in the bar. We are introduced to one another by our names and then by the names of our characters. We sit around the table. Pots of coffee. Conversation strained and polite. I sit beside X. She looks like I've seen her in the movies, except older, thinner. She is on a popcorn diet and munched from a bag on the table before her. There are changes in the script, so we were given new yellow pages with new dialogue. Then our *Direktor* arrived. Tall, about sixty, wearing a floppy hat and tight blue jeans over cowboy boots, he wanted us to read through the script together. 'I just wanna hear the words, I don't want any performances, OK.'

But soon, despite beginning in flat voices, everybody was 'acting', giving it everything.

A young blond actress, beautiful with green eyes, began to cry as she spoke her lines. Nobody looked at her directly, but at the end of her scenes, she looked as if she had heard a silent round of applause.

When it came to my first lines, I was so nervous, I spoke over another actor. This is the one part of acting I can never get used to: those first moments when you are no longer you and you must become the character. I read my lines off the page, cold and flat, but then despite myself I started to invest the words with meaning and feeling, I was now 'acting' too. After, a round of applause for ourselves and the writer, who shifted in his chair, looked at the floor and said, 'Thanks, guys.'

February 9th

We haven't worked yet. The snow continues. We are now relaxed with one another, and people's personalities are beginning to emerge. Tonight an impromptu party in the hotel restaurant. R, the actor from LA, danced up and down the tables as Carmen Miranda, a tablecloth around his waist, holding a fruit bowl on his head as the band played. We all clapped and sang like children, especially the producer who kept shouting 'more, more.'

I have become friendly with N. She is a wardrobe mistress. She is about fifty. This is only her fifth film. She told me her husband was a writer who was denounced as a communist during the McCarthy witch-hunts. She was asked to testify against him. She refused. Neither of them worked in Hollywood again for thirty years. But she doesn't seem to be bitter, only a little nostalgic for the days when she was a young kid in Hollywood and worked with some of the greats like Bogie and Gable. Was her husband back in the business? I asked. 'Yes,' she said, 'but not in movies.' In TV. 'I don't see him very often these days. We split up about two years after the trials.' I said I was sorry. 'C'est la vie,' she said and laughed.

February 10th

In the bar today, V came in. The beauty of this girl amazes me. She asked if she could join me. She smoked unceasingly. We talked for a while. Then she became silent. Then she began to cry. I put my arm around her. Her face was buried in her hands. I tried to take her hands away, but I couldn't. So I just sat there and she lay against me crying. She told me through sobs that the director had just told her that she was not first choice for the role, nor was she the studio's first choice, and that the two actresses they offered it to had turned it down. I told her that wasn't so bad, that a lot of actors got roles that way. I was trying to be reassuring, but I sounded false even to myself. I knew what she was feeling. She had to go through an entire film knowing that every day she walked on the set the director and producers thought her second or third best. I told her the *Direktor* was into control and power and that he was manipulative. She can't let what he says eat away at her belief in herself. I knew what I was talking about, I said. She looked at me for a moment and just looked away again.

February 14th

Next door R plays Ry Cooder tapes incessantly. The girl with red hair who speaks five languages and works in the hotel bar comes to his room most nights. Their lovemaking keeps me awake. It's a kind of torture lying in the dark, hearing and trying not to. Maybe she has a sister!

February 18th

R asked me today if I wanted to borrow his Ry Cooder tapes. I said I'd heard them all before! Then he asked if there was anything else. I said, yes, you could tell Helga to give me a knock some night. He laughed and crossed his eyes. His father is a famous producer, so he grew up in LA as a privileged kid. We get on very well together. I am fascinated by him and the stories of his boyhood in Hollywood. He does a lot of coke. How he gets hold of it here I don't dare to ask him. Once he offered me some. I've enough problems! He says it's amazing for sex. That you can keep it up for hours. So I believe, I said.

February 20th

Nearly three weeks here. Still haven't worked. Have read all the books I brought and am now scrounging paperbacks. A, our star, is being lovely to everybody. But he and the *Direktor* don't seem to be hitting it off according to reports from the nerve centre, i.e. the make-up girls who told me that A called the director an asshole very loudly on the set today.

Out walking in the hills today with U. We saw an amazing sight. About two hundred soldiers in full uniform, guns over their shoulders, skied over the mountain silent and in battalion formation at great speed. We stood watching 'til they disappeared. She said, 'Oh my God, can you believe it?' and flopped down in the snow like a sack of potatoes.

February 23rd

Today R said, 'Can I say something personal?' and I said sure. He told me not to get offended, that I had a good face, but I would have to get something done with the wrinkles round my eyes. I asked him what he was talking about and he said he knew this guy in LA who would do a good job for me. He is only twenty-one, if he doesn't cut this out I tell him, he'll be in some mess by the time he's forty. He really thought he was helping me. Later he apologised. I said to forget it, but I repeated that his head was full of shit and he said yes, I was right.

February 24th

Work today at long last. Short simple scene with no dialogue. Still, the ice had been broken.

Called to A's suite for a rehearsal for the big scene on the train. He answered the door himself. Wearing only a shirt. Trouserless. We sat around the table. A was obviously drunk. The *Direktor* sat on the sofa. A talked while our director listened, and agreed with everything A said. Eventually A said, what do we need this scene for anyway? It's just the same old horseshit between me and what's his name. We've had all this in a previous scene. Who gives a shit?' The *Direktor* agreed with him and said let's cut it.

Then A starts talking about his ex-wife, who broke his balls and took him for every cent he had. 'That bitch,' he said and spilled his drink. We all know who his famous ex-wife is, so we are fascinated, except that suddenly I remembered he's just cut one of my best scenes, and I start not to like this guy who seemingly is a law unto himself. I knew it was pointless to object tonight, but he's not going to push me around. I'm going to talk to the *Direktor*.

A was completely pissed when we left. He kept muttering about his ex-wife and commies and repeating over and over: 'the fast lane, too fast,' whatever that meant. We carried him into the bedroom and laid him on the bed.

February 25th

Relations really strained between A and the *Direktor*. In the middle of scene rehearsal he said to A, 'Could you pick up the pace?' A made a big show of looking round the room behind chairs, and all over the floor. Then he said, 'I didn't know I'd dropped it,' and walked off the set. I felt sorry for the *Direktor*. Soon after A came back on set. He was his usual relaxed self. Meanwhile the *Direktor* had just sat in his chair, flicking over pages of the script. When A returned he got up and continued as before. 'That round to the *Direktor*,' V whispered. A smiled at the *Direktor*. Your problem is you're from the John Gielgud school of acting. Nobody knew what he meant.

February 27th

I spoke to the *Direktor* today. The train scene is back in. Victory!

February 28th

The *Direktor* has been fired. Nobody knows the story yet, but V rang me from the set to tell me the news. I cannot believe it.

February 28th, later

Our *Direktor* has not been fired! Rather he stormed off the set, saying he would not return 'til he got an apology from A. Everything is beyond comprehension. Anything could happen.

Met A in the bar. Very friendly. Showed me a picture of his kids. And a picture of a racehorse. Asked did I know Fairyhouse and Punchestown. Said I couldn't be Irish if I didn't like horses. His new wife loved horses. Loved horses more than people. She hated the movie business, just wanted to be around goddam horses all day. What did I make of that? he asked.

March 2nd

The *Direktor* is back. As if nothing had happened, the movie continues. Nobody knows if an apology has been tendered. What about the train scene?

March 4th

Weather bitterly cold. Now we are working twelve to fourteen hours per day. Everyone high on the adrenalin of the shoot. Nothing else seems to matter. Progress slow because of weather. We have fallen severely behind schedule.

March 12th

Hired a car and went into the country. Just V and me. We had lunch at an old inn. A violinist came to the table and serenaded us. Mostly she talked. She told me she was repulsed about doing the bedroom scenes with A. He had refused even to discuss them with her, just said not to worry, that he would do all the work. It's easy for broads. You just gotta lie there. She said what a disappointment it was to have admired someone like A for years and then you work with them and they are disgusting and drunk and don't give a damn about anything. We went for a walk over a wooden bridge, and stopped before a waterfall. We sat there for a long time just talking. She said, I'd kill myself if you weren't here. I'd die if you weren't in this movie.

March 14th

A refuses to be naked in bed with V. It's in his contract that they cannot shoot below his chest. For the scene he wore three pairs of jockeys. V quite rightly said why should she be naked and he not? 'Have you seen his body?' one of the girls said. 'It's disgusting, all out of proportion. Tiny legs. Long back. And that great flabby hairy ass. Like an ape's.' They all laughed. 'And that belly, yuck! It's out to here,' and she made an enormous circle around herself.

V had to lie naked with her back to camera. She had nothing on, save a G-string. The *Direktor* went crazy. He did an impersonation of her. 'O sure I'll take my clothes off, sure I'll take my clothes off.' Then when it comes to it, she's got this thing on. This thing! And he snapped the elastic of her G-string.

I stopped him. How dare you, I said, treat her like that. She is an actress, not an animal.

March 16th

Rumours that the whole picture is a tax write-off.

March 17th

St Paddy's day. Planxty and wine in my room. Everybody saying Happy St Paddy's day! Crack was 85-90.

March 24th

A and V are having an affair. I cannot believe it. R told me. He insists it's true. Everyone knows. I ask him, for how long? For quite some time, he thinks.

—

Three weeks later, the movie ran into 'financial difficulties', and was never completed. Any similarity to characters living or dead is purely intentional.

A lost night in Venice with
Richard Burton

In 1982, I was asked to play a small part in Tony Palmer's nine-hour biography of Wagner. I accepted for two reasons. Firstly it would be an opportunity to visit several European cities I had never been to before and, more importantly, Richard Burton was playing Wagner.

I had seen him on stage at Oxford University in Marlowe's *Faustus* on a summer's night in 1965. I shall never forget the effect he had on the audience. At the final curtain, as they stood to cheer and roar, there was no doubt that we were in the presence of a great actor. Whatever those much abused words 'charisma' and 'presence' mean, Burton had them to burn. The audience was riveted by him: the poetry and aggression of his movements, the fiery inner intensity and the urgent, mellifluent voice had mesmerised us all.

Nearly twenty years later, as fate would have it, on a snowy January morning in Vienna, I sat nervously on the set of *Wagner*, waiting for Burton to arrive. The scene was a simple one. A conversation between the composer and Karl Ritter, a friend of Wagner. I wasn't the only one who was nervous. There had been rumours of his drinking all weekend. 'He's back on the bloody taste again, the bastard,' I heard somebody high up say. Then suddenly, in a rush of anxious attendants, he arrived.

He was dressed in a bluish fur coat which covered his costume. His face was grey and tired and his shoulders were hunched. He looked as if he was in pain. 'Not a well man,' tut-tutted the executive behind me, as he lit a cigarette, relieved the show was going on at least for today.

'Morning, loves. Let's get to it, shall we?' Burton said to the crew.

The director introduced us.

'Family, really,' Burton smiled. 'Irish and Welsh. How is dear Dublin? I love it. Drank out the bloody Shelbourne more than once.' He winked as the director inquired reverentially if everything was 'Okay, Rich?'

'Don't be nervous, love,' he said quietly to me.

During lunch he spoke about Ireland and about Niall Tóibín and Cyril Cusack, whose work he admired. He had worked with Tóibín in *Tristan and Isolde* and with Cusack several times, including his own production of *The Taming of the Shrew*.

There was wine on the table that day but he drank only Perrier and hardly touched the food. And as on subsequent occasions, he talked and talked of Wales, of rugby, of Dylan Thomas, of Gareth Edwards, Elizabeth Taylor — 'Miss Tits' — and his days as a young actor. 'When I was a windy boy and a bit,' at Stratford, where Kenneth Tynan first said of him as Henry the Fifth, 'A young Welsh boy shines out with greatness.'

He quoted Myles na gCopaleen, Shakespeare, Joyce, Yeats, and smoked Marlboro incessantly.

Few people realised that during *Wagner* he was in great pain, having had operations to relieve trapped nerves in his back. He told me that every morning he had to get up at five o'clock for sessions of gruelling physiotherapy. Towards the end of the film, the pain was so great he had to be hospitalised. His work schedule was punishing. He was in almost every scene. He had to speak volumes of words and locations changed almost every day. He hoped desperately that *Wagner* would be a huge success, as indeed we all did. It wasn't. But he was philosophical about the film business.

'Seventy films I think I've done. We tried to name all the

films I've been in one day for a bet. And we couldn't. I've only seen about ten. Done some awful bloody films, love. You never know that when you begin them. It all depends on the director, the editor. Main thing is, keep working. That's all you can do, really.'

I met him again in Budapest, two months later. Our call was for five-thirty. Even at that time, there were three or four journalists or photographers, shouting questions about whether he and Liz would get back together again. They had been waiting all night.

'Amazing people, journalists. Like wolves,' he said.

It was so cold, one of the photographer's fingers stuck to his camera and they had to cut the flesh off with a penknife.

'Serves him bloody right,' said somebody in the back of the coach.

'Poor bugger, I hope he's all right,' said Burton. He told me that he regretted not being able to move about unrecognised. There were always crowds and he hated crowds. And always the journalists. 'They photographed me on the toilet once!' Yet he was courteous to them. And once I saw him send a round of drinks and an extempore poem to a group of reporters who were waiting outside.

But the abiding image I shall have of him is in the Gritti Palace Hotel in Venice. He had invited four or five of us to his suite for a meal. He was dressed in his customary red (the legacy of a bet he had made years ago with Peter O'Toole), with a black blazer, and he was drinking Pernod. 'My dear old Dad would call me a sissy if he could see me drinking this stuff. Still, I believe it's good for the brain cells.'

Beside him sat a beautiful dark-eyed Italian journalist from one of Italy's leading communist newspapers.

'Doesn't she look like Elizabeth,' said Arthur Lowe.

He was talking to her about money, as he often did, with a kind of childlike amazement. I don't think he ever got over the fact he was a working-class boy from the Welsh Valley who had

made it and had become rich beyond his wildest dreams in a
business that he sometimes disparaged.

Later, I left to stroll around the city before turning in. Venice
by night is full of mysterious and overpowering silence. But
that night, as I returned through the dark empty streets, his
unmistakable voice rang out:

> *And I gave my soul,*
> *A blind slashed eye*
> *Gristle and rind*
> *And a roarer's life.*
> *And I shoved it into the cold black sky*
> *To find a woman's soul for a wife.*

It was Burton, hand-in-hand with the beautiful dark-eyed
Italian. 'The capitalist and the communist,' he said. 'We're off to
Harry's Bar. Come and join us.'

At five o'clock in the morning, we emerged the worse for
wear having witnessed an acting duet, carrying between us
Ekehard Shall, Bertolt Brecht's son-in-law, behind us the journalist who, he later discovered to his horror, had been taping
everything he said.

'Jesus, I filled her with a bottle of Pernod and she's still
straight as a ramrod,' he whispered. At the hotel, the night
porter eyed us warily. 'Give me a stamp,' demanded Burton.

'What price, sir?'

'Any price. Just give it here.' Finally. Shall — the leading
actor of the Berliner ensemble — his room number written in
eyebrow pencil on his forehead underneath a first class Italian
stamp depicting Michelangelo's David was hoisted onto
Burton's shoulder, carried up the stairs and deposited on the
bed of the astonished Mrs Shall. This was the man who said he
couldn't do *King Lear* because he wouldn't have the strength to
carry Cordelia onto the stage.

The last time I saw him was two weeks before he died.
Ironically, he looked better than ever. He had gained weight.

His eyes were clear. He had finally beaten his back ailment. He was talking about *'hiraeth'*, the Welsh word for homesickness. How you never get over it. The pain of exile. 'It's like tearing bits of your skin off every time you leave.' He was still smoking. But he had cut out drinking completely.

I remember thinking to myself on that summer's morning at Twickenham Studios that he had something of immortality about him. People like him were blessed, I was thinking, with an extra life, that he could continue to smoke as he did and still survive. Built like a pit pony and with the lungs of an elephant. In the meantime he had met Sally, his last wife. She had worked on *Wagner* as a production assistant. She was quiet and supportive and they got on terrifically well together.

The so-called Burton entourage consisted only of her and his long-time and devoted friend, Brook Williams, son of Emlyn who had given Burton his first job. He had just bought a house in Haiti and the three were going there to relax before starting three new films. He was happy and was optimistic about *1984*, his last film. Insiders say he is brilliant in the role of interrogator. He was excited about returning to the stage. He was going to do *King Lear*. Definitely. That was a promise. And all the time he talked, the rhythms of his native Welsh tongue underscoring the standard English he learned so hard, with pebbles in the mouth, on the Welsh hillside.

In the time I knew him, I found him caring and approachable, learned, sensitive, witty and a listener with a great curiosity. He was not charismatic simply because he was a star. He was a star because in reality he was charismatic. He had an indefinable difference about him. Something inexplicable, yet obvious to all who met him. It drew people to him because they wanted to share his great warmth.

I feel privileged to have known and worked with him because he was a rare one. I hope that, to paraphrase his hero Dylan Thomas's words, he is lying still, that he is sleeping, that he is becalmed.

Hollywood Lives

The telephone shrills insistent through the rooms of my rented house in Beverly Hills and a recorded voice bids me have a good day. I have lain awake for an hour and watched dawn spill slowly down from the mountains and break grey and dull against my window. Already a thunder of traffic rumbles along the freeways towards Sunset Boulevard and although a watery sun rises, soon day will hang soft and hot, a reddish-brown blanket over this city of angels.

Today is the final day of filming, and we have moved from a huddled town in Europe that clings to the side of a hill to this sunbaked Tír na nÓg. I wait on the sidewalk for my driver. Soon the Mexican gardeners will arrive from their barrio in the east of the city. They carry long steel rods which they sink into the ground to turn on the rain that waters the lawns of the grand houses. Their skins are dark and their faces unsmiling under broad-rimmed straw hats and they go about their work in silence, for they neither acknowledge nor are acknowledged.

The Cadillac is smooth and cool as we glide towards the beach location, through suburbs of rainbow-coloured houses of every conceivable style from French chateau to Tudor to Byzantine, spread out like some kind of bizarre architectural exhibition, all discreetly unhidden behind trees of palm and electric gates. Already the hawkers are sitting on canvas chairs along the green strips between the motor lanes, waving their maps to the homes of the stars at the speeding cars.

At night I have rarely seen the stars. In the sky above, police helicopters beam down lights and whirl angrily away again to wherever they come from.

From my windows I can see the hills. My house is across the canyon from Brando's. The lights come on in there through the trees and sometimes you can see him move about. Jack Nicholson's house is beside that. So close, they could chat across the back wall to each other. My house, they say, was once owned by Betty Grable. I doubt it, but once or twice I fancy I hear her tap dance on the wooden stair.

'How're ye, Betty? You had a great pair o' gams. I just wanted to tell you that. My father called his budgie after you.'

The hills are full of ghosts. Flynn and Bogart, Fairbanks, Gable, swaggering and swash-buckling. The immortals, like the Greek gods, ageless in their celluloid heaven. I am always aware of them and the thrill of being here never leaves me. I see James Stewart one day watering his plants. Jimmy Stewart, for Jasus sake. I mean to say!

At regular intervals tour buses go by. People photograph through the windows the houses of the great ones. The gawkers and the gawked at.

A party at a house high above the city. Liza Minelli singing to Barbara Streisand, Marvin Hamslich playing the piano, Jack Nicholson smiling from a chair, his devil's eyebrow arched.

'Hey, they're just like normal people really,' says my friend, Johnny, from London on a visit. Part of my joy is showing others the fabled city. I recall Michael Caine's mother, a working woman from London, asked by him what she thinks of Hollywood.

'Oh, it's lovely, Michael,' she says, 'but with all this sun, you'd wonder why you never see any washing out.'

My own mother comes to visit. I take her to Chasen's, one of the most famous restaurants. As we enter, we pass the wife of a former president.

'That one's anorexic, I'd swear. She hasn't a pick on her,' my mother says. 'Skin and bone, she could do with a good plate of spuds.'

We are seated at a table in the corner. Bogey's table. She grips me by the arm. 'Don't look,' she says, staring at an elderly but very famous film star. 'It's yer man with the jaw. Yer man, oh God. Imagine him here in this place. I'm not able for it. I wouldn't be surprised *who* walked in. It's like the time Dicky Rock came to the Cherry Tree. Remember? Look, there's that fella off the television. That man's on cortisone, you mark my words. Look at the chin, he didn't get that sucking silvermints.'

She knows more about Hollywood than I do. 'Susan Haywood was buried from that chapel. Very sad life. Just goes to show, money isn't everything,' she says as we pass a church on Santa Monica Boulevard.

I watch my son talk to his mother on a mobile telephone as he walks through Beverly Hills and I think of how different his life is to mine, to my father's. I hear his voice, 'An oul' bicycle wheel an' a stick. That's all we had to play with. Had to walk three miles to school and three back, rain or shine. The only bit o' grub we'd get is a lump of a turnip that you'd pull out of a field. And we were better off. Not like the crowd goin' these days. Too bloody much yez have. That's what's wrong with the world. That's what has yez all gone mad.'

I look up towards the Hollywood sign and smile at the memory of my dear dead Dad who never travelled further than the Aran Islands once for two days. When he arrived back in Dublin, I asked him what he thought of the islands.

'I thought I'd never get back. I don't know how those unfortunates live out there at all.'

Liam Neeson comes over to visit one day. He is gentle and kind and his eyes crinkle when he laughs. We sit by the pool, reminiscing about Dublin and actors we knew then, and the characters and the humour. Laughter and talk, drifting like smoke across the hills. He excuses himself. After a while I wonder where he is. Ellen goes to investigate. She comes to the door smiling, her finger to her lips, bidding me to be quiet. There at the sink, washing the dishes, whistling. The lovely man from Ballymena. We watch him for a long time, lost in his task.

'Here,' I say at last, 'you'll be gettin' me a bad name.'

—

I close my eyes and remember last night's farewell drink with the actors now finished their roles. The famous Polo Lounge, symbol of all that was once glamorous and luxurious about Hollywood, where deals are done, where the walk is walked and the talk is talked, and nobody really knows anything. But who cares? The thing is to be seen to be seen here. We toast each other.

'Great working with you, man.'

'And you.'

'Gotta keep in touch! Y'hear? Y'hear me now?'

Such stuff as dreams are made of! Put money in thy purse, and get the hell out of here, that's my advice. I look around the crowded noisy room.

Two girls are drinking Dom Perignon. One of them has jewels embedded in her fingernails. She leans her face close to the mouth of the other, and listens for a moment, before she laughs deep in her throat, as the candlelight sparkles in her glass. She flicks the glass with her bejewelled nail and a waiter on castors is at the table instantly, head to one side and smiling deferentially. Two black men, eyes glazed like sleepy cats before a fire, watch them. An actor/director whose movies I hate listens to a young man whose hands draw urgent pictures in the air. The actor/director's eyes move constantly, restlessly around the room, 'til they lock with mine for a second, and then they move on. I feel like an escaping prisoner caught for an instant in a beam of searchlight.

I watch him as he wipes his lips with a napkin, black shirt open to display gold chains, a star in a white suit, under which the world famous muscles are bulging and contracting with a life of their own.

How'ya, how's she cutting, ya boy ya!

An actor from London who's famous because of a hit movie two years ago has me pinned to the wall. His hand pushes constantly through his black hair which tumbles onto his forehead. He is on his fifth Scotch and Drambuie with no goddam ice, if y'please, Landlord. He hasn't washed since we began filming, as he believes in the sanctity of body odours. I relight my cigar to cover the pong that escapes from under his stained linen suit.

'So here's the sitch, old fruits. I've signed — gawd, how I hate that word .... Anyway, I've *signed* to do the thingummyjig, the lot, can you believe it? Me!' He makes a noise of mock disgust with his mouth and brays like a donkey.

'Twixt thee, me and yon gatepost, it's seventy-five thousand and if the thing takes off it's, you know, sky's the bloody limit time. Anyway, I goes in and they ask me to read and I do me stchick and I say, you know, this is a serious bloody move for me, maties. I am an actor. I don't do TV. Well, you know, they just sit there and look at me, like I'm from wherever and they say, "But we respect that. We respect you as an artist!" I mean what does *that* mean? "We respect you as an artist!" I mean, *come on.*'

The girl beside him stirs her drink with a little wooden umbrella and sighs a sympathetic sigh. This is his friend Mimi, knows everybody in Hollywood who matters and hasn't worked for four years.

On the radio Sting bids his beating heart be still and Dinty my driver begins his daily ritual of recounting to me the day's news items he has gleaned from his *Weekly World News*. Today it's the model who married a leper, and the corpse whose pacemaker exploded and demolished a mortuary somewhere in Oklahoma, but my favourite is the man whose wife returned from the dead as a goose. Dinty is from New York, but swears

that he is Irish from County Galway, where they got the bay.
His enormous paunch begins at his neck, and he drives with
one hand and talks over his shoulder to me.

'We gotta stick togedde, us Micks, oddewise dem Protesanse
gonna be runnin' the show! Right, Gabe?' Dinty hates Califor-
nia like the good Irish New Yorker he is.

Two months with the length of two long years I have been
here in this déjà-vu city of enigma and paradox and contradic-
tion. A city of mysticism and materialism, of reality and illusion, of incredible wealth and poverty, it defies explanation.
City of palm and jacaranda, tangerine and orange, holly and
wild oak, snow-capped mountains and Santana winds from the
desert. A haven of gurus and false prophets, fortune tellers,
psychic tea-rooms, drugs, crime and, of course, the dream
factory that is Hollywood. Where skyscrapers are few because
of earthquake codes, and buildings are designed to bend not
break, when the dreaded San Andreas fault shifts and the Big
One hits, destroying all, like Sodom and Gomorrah. And shift it
will, for it is not a question of if, but when. Yet never mind, your
dog can have a facial for one hundred dollars a throw, and if
he's depressed can visit the dog psychiatrist, and you can take
him to restaurants where animal food is not served, but 'food' is
served to animals. And around the Greyhound Bus Station, the
submerged population, the derelicts, the released mental
patients, cleared from the streets for the '84 Olympics, queue for
the soup kitchens, helpless and hopeless in this consumer's
paradise. Yet, although the freeways are called arteries, it is the
only city I know without a heart, without a centre, despite the
varied ethnic melting pot of Mexicans, Orientals, Salvadoreans,
Samoans, Lebanese, Armenians, Filipinos and the black ghetto
of Watts that almost died in the tragic riots of '65. If this city has
a symbol it is the automobile, endless snakes of them bumper to
bumper from dawn to dusk, belching fumes into the brown sky.
There are drive-in stores, and drive-in movies, banks and
churches, and of course the ubiquitous gas station. It is not

uncommon for commuters to travel one hundred miles a day, cursing and sweating in endless motor lanes.

We come to a halt on the Santa Monica freeway.

'Gimme Noo Yawk, Gabe, gimme Galway Bay,' and Dinty begins to sing, 'There are some folks who say that I'm a dreamer...'

'We was over there three years ago, and we go in this hotel cabaret, the Jury's, with this guy telling jokes, little guy, glasses. Jeez, he could tell a story this guy! And then we go in the bus again and we go to Kerry and we see all these mountains and stuff. And the Guinness! What a drink. Two o' those babies and I'm singing.'

I try to study my scene but can't help thinking of the man whose wife is a goose. It's a simple scene, just a brief conversation between myself and the leading lady on the beach, but the words swim before my eyes as Dinty drones on. It hasn't been a happy movie to make, though it seems mostly like any other.

'Oh, you should have been here years ago, Gabe. I'm going back now, thirty, maybe forty years. The golden years. LA was a city then. No crime, no violence. Not like you got now. It was paradise. It was like the Garden of Eden. And we couldn't look after the Garden. We destroyed it. We couldn't keep it beautiful.' He shakes his head sadly.

Making films reminds me of those disaster movies where people are trapped on a sinking ship or in a burning building, and the impending disaster forces them to reveal themselves and their real characters in a way they wouldn't normally. Strangers become friends, and friends become enemies and every day is a drama in which people become heroes and cowards and lovers and fighters and lives are lived on fast forward, 'til the movie ends and it's all forgotten and the gigantic importance of it all seems an illusion. So often is the line between reality and fantasy crossed that after a while it is difficult to tell which is which.

'I bet you gonna miss this movie, like a toothache.'

'It's always sad when it ends,' I reply.

The hills are covered with Tintagel mist, here and there dazzling red and yellow blooms splashed against the green, while below the ocean sleeps. In caravan the trucks of the crew are parked along the boardwalk. Only a few fishermen watching out to sea with the patience of sentries, and the long-beaked egrets scurry along the water's edge, hunting food. Wet-nosed dogs explore dunes, ignoring their masters who fast walk from Zuma beach to the end of the land and back before breakfast.

'OK, guys, let's make it a good one.' Our director, insulated against the morning by an enormous pullover with little sheep on it, beats himself with his arms like some kind of beached sea animal.

He puts his arms around my shoulders and leads me away from the others. 'Can I share something with you, Gabe? I gotta tell you, it's been real good working with you, I feel connected with you, as a person, I mean. I just wanted you to know that, OK?

'OK!' I reply. 'Fair play to you. Same here.'

'The shot is simple. She comes towards you, you're like real glad to see her. You kiss, say your spiel, Blah, Blah, Blah, and we track with you, 'til I say cut?'

'Is she here yet?' I ask.

'No. She's probably still meditating or levitating or whatever it is she does. You know our babe, last to arrive, first to leave.'

Late, as she often is, she will arrive apologising as if it were the first time, and the assistant director will kiss her and say, 'Sure, sweetheart, it's cool, we all understand, couldn't be helped.' He will lead her to her trailer, and ask if there's anything she needs. No sense upsetting her today, the last day. Her personal make-up man is Red, part Cherokee, who prefers fishing to films, but is paid to ensure she stays looking her screen age.

'How long's she got?' the producer asked one day.

'You mean today, or in the movies? Six months maybe,' he

says, like a doctor giving bad news to a relative. 'After that, ain't
nothing I can do. You know lately she's been training herself
not to smile, to keep from getting wrinkles.'

I remember a night in Europe ...

—

The population of the town it seems have all removed themselves for the month of August. We, almost, are the only inhabi-
tants of the hotel. Long silent corridors of deep carpet and
chandelier. I am in a suite below her. Often she calls just to talk.
She seems lonely up there by herself. Sometimes I see her on her
balcony, smoking, looking out to sea.

One night I am awoken by thunder so loud, it seems that it
might flatten the hotel. Wires of lightning fork in the night sky.
Rain hammers relentlessly like a drum beat on window panes,
flows in rivers along the drains. I push back the curtain. The
square seems like a gigantic theatrical set.

The phone rings. It is she. 'The storm,' she says. 'Do you hear
it.' She is breathless with excitement. Moments later she knocks
at my door. She has on her long fur coat, her collar up about her
face.

'Come, let's go,' she implores. I laugh at the madness of it.
'Please, let's go. Let's be like children.'

The porter watches us leave, shakes his head hopelessly and
returns to his paper. We are out in the rain that soaks us instantly. She seems like some demented animal in her sodden
coat of fur, her hair matted to her face, eyes wild in the lightning. She stretches her hand to me. 'Let's run,' she implores.

Oh Jasus no, I say to myself. Not running. I desperately try to
remember whether having rubber shoes kills one or saves one
as we move, it seems, in cinematic slow motion through the
wall of rain. Shutters bang violently. Not a soul stirs. All lights
are closed. We are running towards the sea, she pulling me
behind. Initial embarrassment has given way to a feeling of

thrilling excitement as we near the boiling, churning water. For a moment I think that she may insist on jumping in, but when we reach the end of the pier, she throws her sodden arms about me and shouts above the mad wind.

'It's just like the movies, isn't it?'

Oh yes, she is a queer one and I tell you! And me not far behind her.

—

And now she sits in her canvas chair, her name on the back, one of the letters missing. She is silent.

'What's wrong?' I ask.

Tears well in her beautiful eyes and fall, making wet tracks through her make-up.

'I hate this god awful business.'

She turns her face to me. 'You know there's a cinema in London which just shows my movies all day, every day.'

This I did not know, and I look at her and wonder not for the first time if she is insane.

'I'm like God in Europe, they just adore me, but here in this goddam town, you know it's ...' Her voice trails off and she stares into the distance beyond the sea. I lean over and touch her hand.

'I think you're great, and I'm sorry you're sad.'

She looks at me, her eyes become cold, and small sobs shake her body. 'Save it for your close-up, buster. I don't need you to feel sorry for me.' And she walks quickly away, pulling her wrap around her.

So now it's all over, goodbyes said, eternal friendships sworn. The trucks begin to move away, an army on the move again. She kisses me lightly on the cheek, as a child would and says smiling, 'Come up and see me sometime.'

She gives me a package with my name on it written in Olde Englishe lettering. 'Yes, I'll come up and see you sometime. Be good.' The darkened windows of her Rolls close against the day and she is gone.

Later, I open the present. A book. *A Beginner's Guide to God*. As I turn the pages, a photo of her taken ten years ago falls out. She is young now and a beautiful smile lights up her face. Across it is written, 'Love and Light. Fondest Memories, Hollywood. Remember Me!'

The late '80s brought a period of turbulence to my life during which Áine and I separated. I lost my father and shortly afterwards, my younger sister Marian. Then, I moved to New York having fallen in love with a girl from Queens, New York, called Ellen Barkin. We lived in an apartment on Fifth Avenue in Greenwich Village. I was immediately captivated by the city and felt instantly at home and paradoxically alienated. New York gave me freedom and anonymity, and made me feel part of the great river of life in a way I'd never felt before. I was enchanted by its energy and vitality and I began to feel a new sense of optimism and hope about myself and my future. New York along with Ellen allowed me to heal from grief and to become whole again. I was forever walking the streets, giving myself over to the sights and sounds, all new to me.

What follows is a record of a walk on a hot summer's day on Fourteenth Street near where we lived.

The vastness of the city was incomprehensible to me and I felt that if I wrote down my impressions of one street I might perhaps come to understand something of the great city itself.

Noo Yawk, Noo Yawk

'Keep your splendid silent sun / Keep your woods / O Nature and the quiet places by the woods ... Give me the streets of Manhattan'
(Walt Whitman)

Heat pounds the pavement like a hammer. Ninety degrees the weatherman says. The towers of the city shimmer in a breezeless haze.

'Give me a cigarette, you fatass motherfucker.'

'Sorry man, don't smoke.'

Dance off the sidewalk. Polite and fast. Don't make contact. Eyes ahead. Don't show fear. Walk. Don't walk. This way only. One way. No way. Confusion of signs. Eternal orchestra of sounds. Horns and hooters. Subway shaking the sidewalk. Above the Lone Star Café a sixty-foot iguana, ball-bearing eye, tail-tip broken, threatens to swallow all.

Yeah, welcome to Fourteenth Street. You got it my friend. Fifty dollar shirt only five! Twenty-five dollar suspender pants only three! Streets of the fake Rolex. Tweety Bird clocks. Home of the hanging basket and candy floss in plastic bags.

A child floats seven balloons, seven silver hearts high in the air about the heads of the passersby. Stop for a snow cone, translucent shavings planed from a log of ice stuffed in a paper-cup with syrup poured all over. Pay the barrowman a dollar.

Move on through the blanket of heat. Along the sidewalk sentries perch on ladders above the crowds. 'Big sale.' 'Big sale.' 'Check it out.' 'Check it out.' 'Discount.' 'Discount.' 'Come on in.' Over and over the mantra rap repeated, eyes scanning crowds like electronic cameras for thieves and buyers.

By a railed tree, caged-in flowers at the base, a white-robed Nubian displays his books, touches his lace skullcap in blessing. Black face so calm, so kind. 'Was Christ really crucified?' he gently asks. 'Was Saint Paul disciple or deceiver? And who was Marcus Garvey?'

I shrug and move away, feeble smile of apology he must have seen a thousand times today.

In a doorway a beggar holds his bowl. 'Just one penny, just one penny' a sign beside him reads. 'I am hungry, I am homeles, anything will help, please, thank you.'

'Don't you know there's another "s" in homeless?' a lady scolds before she drops a dime.

'Oh yes, ma'am, I know that. The other "s" just wouldn't fit on my sign, is all.' She sniffs and passes on, not believing.

At the crossing, by the traffic light, two brown shoes taped with bandaid left and lonely, as if their owner just stepped out of them and walked away. Barefoot on the sidewalk.

Further on, two men. Eyes locked in rage.

'You come here again I'm gonna choke you, motherfucker.'

'I don't steal your goddam patch.'

'You hear me now. Don't come here no more.'

'Oh I am scaaared! Nigger.'

'Who you calling nigger, you goddam spic? Show me where you white, white, W-H-I-T-E. Show me lil bit of white on your whole motherfucking body.'

Between the buildings, empty space enclosed by wire. A wasteland. Broken umbrella like an uprooted flower beside a rustled hubcap. Peels of orange, old newspapers, butts of cigarettes, bamboo sticks. Over there gilt frame of a painting, a lady's wig. A paper cup that says 'I love New York' in red. In the corner a tree is slouched like a drunk against the graffitied wall. A silver sign burning to the touch: 'Please keep Fourteenth Street clean.'

Here, the Hope and Grace Mission, 'Christ died for our sins.' Next door the Variety Playhouse is showing *Little French Maid* (she was born to serve!) and *Marathon* (they gave a party and everybody came!). The man outside rattles a keychain. Winks. His teeshirt says 'Life's a bitch. Then I married one.' Into the dark of Dan Lynch's bar. Who is Dan Lynch? Christmas lights and holly adorn the walls, air conditioning rumbles loud as the mail-boat engine. Broken fan hangs useless from the blue cracked ceiling. Ella sings sweet on the jukebox. 'The strong gets strong, the weak just fades, empty pockets don't ever make the grade.'

Pictures of soul singers. Ads for Rolling Rock beer and McSorley ale. Coloured framed photo of a man before a barbed wire fence. White space underneath it says 'Dan Lynch — 1931-1984'.

A huge Alsatian stretched behind the bar starts suddenly awake. Between the bottles on the shelf, a plastic Elvis. Beside me, red and white of the Budweiser sign flicking on and off in his glass, an Irishman. Unmistakable. Cap set back on head, tricolour in lapel. We embark on the ritual questions and answers of Irishmen who meet abroad. He is set for an orgy of nostalgia, but I finish my beer and leave.

Out of the dark and into the light. They are tearing up flag-stones and the noise is like pain. The flagstones are broken and the clay is dried almost at once under the sun that has no mercy. Children play and splash in water fountains that spray from the fire hydrants and water stains the road and sweeps the junk before it to the drains.

In the pet shop where violaters will be eaten alive, they say, 'Hey, man, man, don't overwind the mechanical mouse.' Why? 'Because it hurts, is why!' Here live the upside-down catfish, the needlenoses, flying foxes, midnight angels and the sailfin mollies.

Darting iridescent jewels. Colours of sky and silver and blood. They live in toy motor cars in tanks of glass filled with water. For months I have never seen the grey lizard blink. He lies still as a stone. And even the tapping of the children's fingers cannot move him.

From a blue kaftan the saxman removes his sax. Handles it like a child. Blows and tunes and spits. Throws a quarter in a cardboard box. To start the ball rolling so to speak. Softly begins 'A Nightingale Sang in Berkeley Square'. Above him, faded gold of gargoyles, and pigeons call from balconies. I sit on some steps and listen. Hard. As I must do often here to tell which sounds are which, for so easy do they all become as one. Sneezing of buses. Squeal of brakes. The helicopters' whirl. The banshee wail of the paramedics' van. The high-rise bell that tells the hour at five. And somewhere the tinkly theme of Mr Softee plays 'Waltzing Matilda'.

The day begins to lose its heat. Behind a terracotta lion, a real grey city cat watches on. One eye lidded from a fight.

Fourteenth Street Subway. Path trains to New Jersey, Downtown and Brooklyn. The wind from underground comes in sudden fetid breaths, making women hold their dresses as they pass through the yellow ribs of the exit gates.

'Give a dime to an old trooper.'

'Sorry, no change.'

'*You're* sorry? I'm sorry I asked.'

'Hey, Rosie, you're looking good.'

'I'm not Rosie.'

'You sure? Well, you still pretty.'

A busker curses a broken string. A bag lady, tinselled garland in her hair, tells herself a joke.

In Union Square Park a child is chasing pigeons over the sunbaked grass. They wheel and turn low over the seats where people sit, making them bend their heads.

'Hey, I don wan dem mudders comin in mah face.'

A squirrel in nut heaven watches for nut robbers. A girl

sleeps under a maple tree. *Steppenwolf* open on her lap, as the wind turns the pages. Sandals beside her painted toes. Hair hiding the palest face. And from among the roses Paul Revere weathered green salutes Fourteenth Street from a charging horse. Voices drift on a shifty wind.

'Where you come from?'

'Caracas. Yes. Caracas.'

'Where that?'

'Venezuela. Yes. Venezuela.'

'What you got there?'

'Thermal. Here. Thermal underwear.'

'How much you pay?'

'Two dollar fifty.'

'You come back in the winter. See if you get thermals two dollar fifty, man.'

'You can get a overcoat for a dollar today. See. 'Cause today is probably the hottest day of the goddam year. You know what I'm saying, my friend?'

Silence between them now. Over there, the shoe shine man is making mirrors of leather. With soft rags.

Time to drift back, through shadows and pools, by a hymning church and a hallway smelling of spice. Stand a moment. Watch the crane. Huge metal ball, with the slowest of motion, is swinging towards target. The face of a wall is torn away and the floor of a parlour gapes through. Blue spotted wallpaper and timber and brick. The crowd gathers round to watch the death of a house. Perpetual change is the fate of the street. Streams of cars, every mode of transport on the cratered roadway. Rollers and limos, skateboards and bikes, fleets of yellow cabs, trucks, buses and the creak of a horse-drawn carriage.

Please don't keep looking up, Johnny Appleseed, at the towers of crystal and steel hiding their heads among clouds. The muggers will know you're not native and make you their target. But I cannot keep my eyes from them day or night. The skies swim in glass and clouds pass from window to window and how the sun distorts itself in these challengers of scale. These thieves of light. And behind each window, a story, a life.

The manholes spit steam. Vagrants search the trash cans. The lights come on in million-dollar apartments. Shadows lengthen as evening comes falling, covering corners and ledges and steps and all the secret places: changing the shape of things, filling the spaces between buildings, and moving slow as time over all the streets of the city.

Return of the Quiet Man

When I return to my hotel, there is a phone call. A friend of mine is leaving for the States on holiday and wonders if I'd come to spend a month at his cottage in Ireland.

'Come play the Quiet Man,' he says. For real. Because there is an ongoing strike in Hollywood I accept at once and book a flight for the following day.

'Well you can tell the party of the first part that I go for it.'

The rattling train from Dublin defeats sleep and three hours later I step onto the platform at a tiny station in a shower of early evening rain.

'A fine soft day in the spring it was when the train pulled into Castletown and himself got off.'

The tarpaulin on the roof of the bus flaps wildly in the wind and sunlight hits the window giving it a mad flashing eye, as it charges over the hill towards us.

We climb aboard, an old man in a cap with a twine shopping bag and myself. We swing out of the town into the blue-black hills. The old man sways towards me holding the seats to steady himself. 'Are you who I think you are?'

'I hope I am who you think I am.'

He thrusts a pencil and a torn cigarette packet in my hand.

'What name will I write?'

'Your own of course.' A reprimand. 'Are you down making a film or what?'

'No, just holiday.'

'And other things, Mickeleen. Other things.'

Now and then, the doors of the bus open in a hissing sound and without losing speed, bundles of newspapers are thrown to land on pavement or gravel or in shop doorways. Down the hill, and the last of the day dying, to halt finally under a sign that says 'CIE' swinging rusty in the wind.

The clock on the townhall tower is stopped forever at 12:20 exactly, and under it a group of men are smoking and playing pitch and toss.

They stop to watch me, the stranger among them. The bus turns and heaves itself back up the hill, canvas still flapping madly over the hedgerows. I approach the men, purposefully. I enquire of them the whereabouts of my friend's cottage.

'Christ, you've a step to go yet. You've a right to go over to Kelly's and root out the Vampire. He has a sort of taxi.' They laugh.

'Can you tell me the way to Innisfree?'

'Innisfree is it?'

'Happen you know the road to Aughanure?'

—

At the bar a man who looks as if all the blood has been drained from his body is watching *An Nuacht*. On the TV, Yasser Arafat smiles into a microphone.

'You see that hoor with the dishcloth on his head? That's a crafty hoor if ever I seen one.'

We shake hands. I offer him a drink.

'Well that being the case, it is a pleasant evening and I will have a drink, Sean Thornton.'

'So you'll be staying out at the Lake House, far from the maddening crowds is it? A blowy spot but if it's peace and quiet you're after, no better place.'

'Innisfree?'

'This way!'

It begins to rain again. Long nails of rain in the carlight. The rubber from the windscreen wiper is missing and it scrapes across the glass. Dave Fanning talks low on the radio. Suddenly, without warning, two white ponies stand in the roadway before us staring us to a swerving standstill. Dave Fanning's voice fills the night, and my heart is exploding in my chest.

Further on, cars are parked outside a football field. Men lean against them with shoulder bags and hurleys, staring and saluting as we pass. A man in a vest is frozen momentarily by the headlights, one leg in his underpants, his backside bare to the night. The Vampire rolls the window down as the man dances for cover.

'By Jasus Finnegan, you've a lovely arse, God bless it.' The journey seems endless.

'The young May moon is beaming love, the glow-worm's lamp is gleaming love.'

'It's a good job you can't see where we are now,' says the Vampire.

'Why is that?'

'Oh, that's why,' he laughs.

At last we arrive. A light shines from the cottage set among trees. We part on a handshake.

'Tis a nice soft night. I'm thinking I'll go and talk a little treason with my friends. Goodnight, Mickeleen Óg. Goodnight, Sean Thornton.'

I find the key under the stone by the door. A fire flames in the grate in a crooked blue room. Sleep comes fast in a settle bed.

I awake to the morning and call of birdsong, and a wind that moves the trees outside the window. These only disturb the stillness and I realise that these sounds have become alien to me, and I must learn to listen again.

I open the door of 'White O'Morn' to the garden and a wooden gate that gives onto a sloping field of dandelion and daisy. And beyond this the lake. The water is a sheet of grey glass furrowed by tiny waves that break regular as breathing among the tall reeds. A scatter of swans moves slow in the still day, and a heron flies heavy-winged above.

The hills beyond the lake lie like dark cats waiting to pounce. There is something dangerous, threatening about them, even in sunlight as they cast shadows and take on the moods of sky and water.

Of course I am aware that my stranger's eyes see it so, but still it is not the chemically coloured Innisfree of a film director's romantic imagination. And I am victim to the fallacy that this landscape has always been thus. It is pagan and timeless, yes, but the only constant in any landscape is change, however imperceptible. And so for a time I feel I belong here, for there are times when the feeling of being part of a landscape is greater than the sense of being outside it.

On my walks I notice everywhere small battles between growth and decay, between man and nature. The nettle that grows solitary from a concrete wall. The Massey Ferguson abandoned in the corner of a field, grass growing in the gearbox. The hare that starts from under a broken boat, a waddle of ducks bending under a rusting gate.

By the railway track, unused now, for many miles I walk 'til I come to the station house. A ruin, where rooks have built their nests and groundsel grows in the waiting room. And if I look to the distance, it's Sean Thornton I see, his face as dark as the black hunter he rides along the tracks to the waiting train. And she, Mary Kate Dannaher, with her freckles and her temper and her flame red hair, leaning out the carriage window as she waits for him.

'Don't go, Mary Kate. You've married a better man than you know. 'Tis Sean Thornton loves you surely.'

And he kisses her upturned mouth as the smoke of the engine swirls about them.

'Oh, there'll be no bolts or locks between us, Mary Kate, only the bolts and bars of your mercenary little heart.'

A shutter on a broken hinge bangs closed.

Across the boreen from the cottage there is a wood, dark and

mysterious. Easy to imagine Gráinne against a tree there asking
Diarmuid if a droplet of water on her white thigh is more brave
than he. And among damp grass, splashed with wildflower
there are paths that meander drunkenly, yet logical and ancient
as the trees themselves. In this, the most secret and pagan of
places, the peace of a chapel pervades. Once, surrendering to a
delinquent urge to shout out, I am immediately shamed with a
feeling of desecration. This wood is for silence, or at the most for
whispers only.

Hours I spend in the garden, watching the beginning of lilac
and apple-blossom, pink and white ignite in the branches of a
fallen tree. Through an ivy-covered break in the wall, a view of
the lake beyond. Behind an outhouse, plum trees have been
planted and everywhere bees hang in the bells of flowers. Now
is the season for nettle soup, but a poem about nettles by Peter
Fallon haunts me still and I cannot think to pluck them.

My nearest neighbour lives across a field in a mobile home,
sheltered by the ruins of his former house. An old Bosch fridge
door serves as his gate and in the pathway, in rain or shine, his
old rag of a dog lies sullen and sad, dreaming of long ago sheep.
He talks across the hedge to me with the shyness of a child.

'You that's been abroad, what would you think of this place
now?' He offers me a Silvermint and watches me under his
eyebrows. Between the peak of his cap and his forehead is a
birthmark of red skin. Once, he tells me, he caught a great black
bird, a stranger to the lake, bringing it down with a single shot;
dragged it home and tied it to a post with ropes, 'til it died
screeching a week later. At night he comes with poteen and he
talks of a brother beyond in America.

'Cincinnati?'

'No. Pittsburgh.'

'Oh aye, Pittsburgh, Massachusetts, where the steel and pig iron
furnaces are so hot a man forgets his fear of hell.'

We talk of *The Quiet Man* and the little fella with the horse
called Napoleon and Maureen O'Hara giving lip to John Wayne

and the way he put his shoulder to the door in the storm and it broke under the weight of them. 'That was a great pitcher. Very true to life,' he laughs.

More poteen in his blue mug.

'I never married, no, I suppose I was kinda choosey, and the Mother, God be good to her, wouldn't hear of another woman in the house. Sure everyone has some fad or *mí-ádh* on them. That was mine I suppose. When we were childer we came visiting in this house and we'd sit in the corner there by the fire and look up the chimney and count the stars.'

Máire is his sister, a tiny timid woman who never speaks and moves like a ghost between the caravan and the fields. She hides her hands under a spotted apron and they move in there like little trapped birds.

'There are some things a man can't forget, Mary Kate.'

'Like what, supposin'?'

'Oh the sight of a girl in a field with the sun on her hair.'

On Sunday I go to Mass. The men stand outside the railing 'til the last bell calls them in, stamping out their cigarettes which they hold under their palms away from the wind. The chapel smells of damp. I stand at the back among the late-comers, the women in scarves, the men kneeling on handkerchiefs to protect Sunday suits. After the silence of the Consecration, an explosion of coughing and then the slow eye-roving procession to Communion. I walk the three miles home, passed by men on bicycles who say morra, and cars stuffed with gawking children beep their horns in salutation to the stranger among them.

I stop at the shop named Open and buy the papers from another world and cigarettes for the long Sunday afternoon in the room where the clock made in Romania ticks crazily backwards.

—

It is time for me to leave. There will always be the coming and the going, the breaking of camp, the journey towards something else. The goal is always another place.

I have lit the room with candles that shiver in the draught from underneath the door and throw my shadow huge across the walls. I will miss hearing the chimney winds and the spitting of rain against the crooked window and the drip of it from the thatch. And outside in the darkness, the bleat of sheep and the call of wildbirds and the twisty fingers of trees against the sky. Tonight clouds cover the stars, but as always you watch for one that falls and tells a soul to heaven goes. No house light shines in the distance, but only some pulse of yellow light unknown to me, flickering in the trees beyond the lake.

Are the swans sleeping now? And the cows, immobile as ornaments all day, gone happily home? Have the ponies galloped away beyond the hills?

'Living in a shack near the slag heaps, White O'Morn and Innisfree came to mean a little bit of heaven, Mickeleen Óg.'

Now and then a dog is barking but if I listen now, the silence answers back across the water and along the fields of night.

I keep it all like a movie hidden in the vault of memory, to be screened at will, at any time of day or night, wherever my road may take me.

1984: I landed the role of Christopher Columbus in a gigantic American production. My co-stars were a who's who of the movies: Faye Dunaway, Max Von Sidow, Rossano Brazzi, Virna Lisi, Oliver Reed, Nicol Williamson. We filmed in the West Indies, Spain and Malta, and the US press described me as 'a hunk soon to be discovered by the women of America'.

Christopher Columbus has been described as somebody who, upon embarking on his journey, didn't know where he was going; who, when he arrived there, didn't know where he was; and who when he returned, didn't know where he had been. A fairly accurate description of myself at the end of nine gruelling months

Shangri-La in Ferment:
Post-Columbus Santo Domingo

It had been a long flight. Ten hours from London via Miami and Haiti.

'Excuse me, sir,' said the immigration official. 'You will enjoy our beautiful country, yes?' His signature was a tight ball of barbed wire across my visa. He handed back my passport. 'Welcome to Dominican Republic,' he smiled.

My knowledge of the Caribbean was hazy and predictable, heavily influenced by tourist sales talk and too many pirate films in the Carlton. However, thanks to Eoghan Harris I was aware of the history of exploitation and slavery and the strategic and geo-political importance of the area as a link between the Americas. But it still seemed a kind of romantic place, a tropical Shangri-La of exotic islands, peopled by unself-consciously outgoing natives.

'Mr Columbus,' said a voice behind me. (In this business you get used to answering to different names.) 'My name is Ramón. How you do?' He was a small man in a dirty straw hat. He was to be my driver for the next five months.

Through the open window, the breezeless night smelled of eucalyptus and behind the palm trees and the hoardings the sea seemed to be asleep. On the radio, the headlines announced that the President would be meeting Mr Reagan at the White House to discuss the island's economic future and its important relationship with the US. A fingernail of a moon raced us all the way. In the bar of the Hilton, Ramón handed me a letter.

'They ask me give you this.' The Johnny Bennett trio merangued discreetly in the background for an unheeding scattering of tourists, drinking piña colados and Jack Daniels. A beautiful mulatto girl, who had been sitting with two men, moved to a table by herself and smiled directly at me. I opened the letter.

'Instructions From The Company Regarding Travel and Location' and in capital letters, 'WELCOME TO SANTO DOMINGO. PS Beware of VD.' I looked up. The girl was still smiling.

The location at Portillo was five-and-a-half hours from Santo Domingo, along a red-brown dirt road with sugar cane and tobacco plantations stretching away on either side to the horizon. In the fields we saw the workers. Men and women bent under the scorching sun.

'Three-quarters of our people have no land,' Ramón told me. Later I was to discover that in the Dominican Republic most arable land is divided between multinationals and powerful landowners.

The windowless houses of the villages through which we passed were of grey untreated wood. I was reminded of the huts for Palestinian refugees at Jericho. Through the open doors, photographs and advertisements cut from women's magazines decorated the walls. But there was no furniture save for makeshift tables and beds and no covering on the earth floors. Old men sat smoking in rocking chairs and children played in the yards among the hens and scrawny dogs.

Heat at last gave way to the chill of the late afternoon and the light began to creep slowly from the fields. The roadways were crowded with the labourers returning on foot from their work. I had never seen so many people outside a city before and thought that Ireland must have been as poor and as crowded as this in the days before the Famine.

We stopped to drink by the roadside. An old leather-faced woman used her machete to split open a coconut, which she offered to us as the milk ran between her fingers.

At about three o'clock in the morning, we arrived at the little village, which was to be our home for the next five months. Our house was palm-covered, with bedrooms and a kitchen. Soon I fell into a deep sleep. I was awakened by the feel of something itching my face. It was a great black insect with enormous feelers about the size of a finger. I could not go back to sleep.

The following day I was confined to bed with a tropical fever consisting of shakes and shivers, grotesque nightmares in which old forgotten schoolteachers came back to haunt me. My throat was so swollen I could not swallow. I was given injections, antibiotics, tablets and because illness is not a word producers like to hear on film sets, I was sent back pale and weak and high as a kite from medication to discover the New World.

Although the heat was almost unbearable and an Italian actor playing a swarthy cut-throat collapsed of heat stroke, we worked on. The crew in bathing trunks, the actors baking in fifteenth-century doublets and coarse woollen tights.

Our boats carved from tree trunks, like the originals, nosed towards the shore. Behind us, an exact replica of the *Santa Maria* lay at anchor. Despite the heat, a feeling of intense excitement gripped us. We were re-enacting one of the most important events in the history of the world in almost the exact spot where it had occurred.

It was easy to imagine the moment when their boats thudded onto the hot white sand for the first time. The Spaniards had splashed through the water towards the naked Indians, swapping bits of broken crockery, barrel hoops and hawk belts for the gold the natives wore around their necks.

They threw themselves at the feet of their conquerors, who they believed had come from heaven. And the Admiral, having kissed the ground like the Pope, unfurled the standard of Ferdinand and Isabella and declared the island a possession of the kings of Spain and Jesus Christ. When the Indians wore the shining blades and daggers of the Spaniards, they cut themselves through ignorance on the edges, knowing no other weapons except bone harpoons and spears made of cane.

Owing to bad lighting and sound, and the countless other things that go wrong when filming, I began to lose some of my sense of wonder after the third take. Great discoverers arrive only once. And kiss the ground only once. But after Take Fourteen of wiping sand from my lips, I had begun to loathe the place — and Columbus himself for not landing somewhere more convenient like New York. And preferably by plane.

I used to think of Columbus as being simply an explorer, the great navigator who discovered America in 1492. But he was more than this. He was also a fanatical and devout Catholic, a murderer and a cultural imperialist who believed in the expansion of Spain, and the spread of the Catholic faith at any cost. He brought back not only gold and silver, peppers and other exotic fruit, but also slaves for the markets of Spain. I also soon learned that for Indians he is a devil, not a hero, and that we were not here to tell that story but to distort history once more.

Quickly the routine of filming was established. And as always a small intimate world of our own was created. It was as if the outside world did not exist and we had been there forever. Now and then a small plane would arrive, carrying month-old newspapers and post. One day I noticed a group of extras dressed as Spanish soldiers hunched around a transistor. They began to speak excitedly.

Slowly we began to understand what was happening. The government, in order to secure a loan from the International Monetary Fund, had been told to tighten the screws in the Dominican Republic. A huge rise in food prices had been announced. The people, already broken by appallingly high prices for essentials, could take no more and had begun to riot and loot the shops. Rumour countered rumour: the soldiers were shooting on sight and fifty people had been killed that morning. Later, the numbers of dead would soar; villages were being burned; the Americans would invade just as they had in Grenada.

'They keep us in political quarantine because they fear infection from Cuba,' said Ramón. The Americans were using the IMF loan to provoke the situation. The puppet government was rounding up and imprisoning people at random. 'We have nobody to speak for us,' he said. 'Even the Church has abandoned us.' The airport was closed. Nobody could leave the country. Curfew was imposed. Soon it would reach Portillo and we would all be killed.

Spirals of black smoke rose behind the hills and somebody shouted *'Viva la Revolucion!'*

The producers were calmly anxious, but insisted that the most important thing was to finish the film. Suddenly the safe intense world we had built was shattered and the film seemed to me to be not the most but the least important thing. I felt that what we were doing was meaningless in this context. And I wondered what relevance the sanitised story of Columbus would have among these people who used machetes instead of tin openers.

Two days later, with shooting miraculously complete, we stood on the weed-covered runway, waiting for a twin-engined plane to airlift us to Santo Domingo airport. The roads were too dangerous for travel, and the minibus bringing a German actor to the set had been overturned and set on fire.

As we climbed into the sky, I saw Ramón wave his hand just once in a kind of blessing and walk quickly back to his old jeep.

Down low we could see telltale signs of smoke in the scattered villages and soon we arrived at Santo Domingo.

In the souvenir shop, I bought some jewellery made of amber — a petrified, fossilised resin, millions of years old. Inside the beautiful gem, insects were trapped. As we waited for take-off, I thought it was a meaningful souvenir of a poor, tormented island and its people trapped like insects in its beautiful shape.

Minutes later, we were out over the sea, heading for Madrid.

A Final Performance

I took Ellen back to Ireland, which she loved though she was adamant about never wanting to live there. We spent a great deal of time in Dublin. I remember an evening at the home of Shay Healy. A special, magical evening for me. Enjoying my wife's enjoyment, laughing and listening to Dublin yarns. Paul Brady sang a haunting song about Elvis.

Shay's father, old and frail now, sitting by the fire, was called upon. And rising from the depths of his soul came the mysterious and powerful energy of the actor as he began to recite 'Dawn on the Hills of Ireland'. In a way it was his story, of his boyhood in Kerry, of leaving and returning. Out of that frail body came a passion and a thunder which I can never forget. It was his final performance perhaps and we were privileged to witness it.

And later as I remembered his words and replayed the scene in my mind, I began to write the following piece called 'Coming Home'. I offer it to his memory.

Coming Home

Brooklyn Bridge is a necklace of lights
over the river turning in troubled sleep
as we sleek silent
in the bruised half-light of New York evening.
Rags of birds hang on winter wires
and without the window of our car,
the secret city passes by.

And you and I,
separate now in the hidden rooms of our hearts;
a fingernail of moon
raced us all the way to Fifth and Twenty-first
and then —
like paper that is blown against an instep,
the memory of an evening that is passed —
an actor, old and holy as a prayer
freed from the tabernacle of his soul
the trapped birds of memory and song.
And joyously they winged among the listeners
by a fire dying in a green room.
Called up for us then, his ancient boyhood hills,
and fields of Kerry
and a homecoming dawn in a once upon a time.
Sang for us a song of lonely leaving
and time's sad turning.
And I thought then the curse of age
is memory. Of youthful days, forever with us.
And as his poemsong stilled, a voice,
his younger self beside me said
'Fair play to you, Da,' under a thunder of applause.
And turning to you then I saw
that you were moved as I
knowing this forever moment we would keep
like a photograph we treasure
wherever our days or ways might take us.

Into the West took four years to reach the screen. That it ever did is due to a great extent to the persistence of Tim Palmer, its producer. It was he, with his friend Michael Peirce, who first had the idea to make a film about a white horse and the Travellers.

I was living in New York at this time (1987) and they asked me if I could help get it made. I urged them to contact Jim Sheridan — then an unknown in movies — to write the screenplay. He did, wonderfully, but we still couldn't get the picture fully financed.

Eventually, my agent at ICM, Andrea Eastman, fixed a meeting for me with Bob and Harvey Weinstein at Miramax Films. I told them the story of the two brothers and the white horse over lunch, and they agreed to come in for the rest of the finance.

In collaboration with several other sources, such as Channel Four and Littlebird, the cameras finally rolled in the winter of 1991, during the worst weather for many years.

And I got to know many of the Travellers: one of them a man for whom I have special regard. His name is John McDonagh.

This is his story, in his own words.

The Traveller

Although the sun is weak, the traveller shields his eyes against its pale light. The inside of his hand is hard in handshake. His welcome is warm. We are friends for months now. He leads me by a yard of broken cars and prams and a million rusted things. A cock on one leg watching with fierce curiosity. 'Elvis,' nods the traveller. 'We had a hen called Madonna but she's dead now.' The traveller is famous for his love of animals.

'Put a cup of tea before the man,' he orders one of his children as we enter the rough and ready caravan and not the fancy one. 'On the side of the road I was born. In a tent. Out where the Saw Doctors come from in the town of Tuam. Eight brothers I had. And the girls. Cathleen one, Teresa two, Bridie four, Anne six, Ellen five — how many's that?

'Monivea, Athenry, Clancy's Wall, Ryhill, Corofin, my oul' father travelled that county. He never moved away from Galway in the line of travelling wise. And I went to school to learn my prayers is all. To make my Communion and Confirmation. For I had no interest in the reading and the writing and I don't miss it. I'm not saying it's not a gift to have it but I know every road there is to know out there to the County Mayo and back. There's not a road in Ireland that's strange to me.

'Picking spuds and pulling beet or picking stones in any road, them's the only jobs I had in them days. In all weathers, come rain come shine. You'd get a half crown from a farmer and it was eight of them to make a pound note. But I seen myself eating green mouldy bread and I'm not ashamed to say it. And my mother crying because she had no money to feed us — them's facts.

'And the wheel of a bike you'd have and beat it with a stick up and down the roads, and an oul' wireless up in the wagon. That was the time of the wet battery and the dry battery. Do you remember? That was our entertainment in them days. The only thing that we would listen to was the *seanchaí*, and Din Joe and there might be half a dozen inside and another crowd outside. For there was no television in them days. That's a thing I don't agree with for young children. And it's not the violence I'm coming at, but women taking off their clothes and getting into bed with men that's not their husbands.'

A beautiful brown-eyed girl of seven or eight watches him, her father. 'Take her away from me,' he says to one of the others gathered about him. But they pay him no heed.

'And then I got married. Do you see that lad there?' He nods towards a handsome boy of fifteen or sixteen years. 'He's getting married this summer. Do you know why travellers get married young? Because they die young. Them's facts. Anyway, I tell you about that crack. I sold a horse to get married. I hopped on a train one fifteenth of August. It was the blessing of Our Lady's Well, I remember, and I had the few shillings saved. Off with me to see an uncle of mine. "For what are you over, John?" says he. "I'm going to get myself a woman," says I. I had her picked out you see — for every man has a corner in his eye for one woman and that oul' one of mine I knew her since she was a child, so I lifted her out of the blue.

'But my father was like a spitting divil. "Where were you, mad John?" says he. They call me that because I do stupid things,' explains the traveller. ' "I was above in Athenry looking for cattle," says I. "What sort of cattle?" says he. "Cows," says I, for I knew my father was agin me, you see. In the heel of the hunt I ran away with her from Athenry to Tuam. We walked along the railway track, avoiding the roads 'til we came to Gill's

Public House. And I stole a bike there and put her up on the front of it and the chain broke, and didn't I get locked up for a couple of days in the barracks before we got married, for getting drunk.

'Well, the job was done in the wind up, a Claddagh she had on her finger and that cost me seventeen and six pence, we've been together ever since. Thirty years, the length we've been together now.'

The windows of the trailer are closed tight and the smoke from his cigarettes hangs still and heavy in the air. Between pulls, the traveller looks at me. There are secrets behind his blue eyes. Secrets he will never tell me.

'Me and her went to the pictures that night with a sister of mine. Clint Eastwood was in it. An oul' thing. He was only a young boy in it. There was a bit of a rooly booly that night and a few gallons of porter. But we had no honeymoon. Settled people will do that, but the oul' traveller works in a different way.

'Anyway a few weeks later, her mother gave the money for me and her to go to England. I waited in England then 'til 1967, working the oul' building sites or gathering the scrap, you know the crack. I lived in a house there, but I was in it agin my will, but the people in that country, Liverpool, are all right. They gave us respect for they're decent people if you work them right. If you play the game with them, they'll treat you fair. And the other crowd that won't go agin you is the blacks. They'll call you "Paddy", doesn't matter what your name is as long as you're Irish. Well I never minded what they called me. Call me "Paddy", call me "Tinker" or "Gypsy", but don't call me "Knacker". Because a knacker is a dead horse, if you don't know.

'Well you miss your own in the end and back we come with two children, the John fella was an infant and the Mary wan was walking. And here in Ireland we've been ever since. But if I had my own will, and I'll say it from the top of a mountain, if I had to live the way I wanted to live, I'd live in the town of Athlone. They're the most hospitaliest people that I ever came across, people that'll call you into a house and give you a cup of tea, make no differ if you're a tinker or not.'

The traveller leans forward. He points towards houses beyond his window.

'You'd liefer put a bird in a cage than put me in one of those. Them's facts. For if you gave me down one of them, I'd leave it for the birds in the air. That's the way I am. The way my oul' father was. And his father before. There's no changin' that. It's in the blood.'

It's getting dark outside and objects are beginning to lose their shapes. The sky is heavy with rain.

'And I'd live where you'd die,' says the traveller. 'A fox in a hole. And I'd see what you don't see and I'd get what you couldn't. Where you'd buy one loaf of bread, I'd buy twenty for the same money. For I know places you don't know, and I'm not being ignorant with you, but you have your own little ways of thinking and we have ours and that's the way of it. I'm a travelling man and I'm a happy man. And a man should live his own life.

'I enjoy doing what I'm doing. For when I'm drinking, I'm drinking and when I'm looking for a living, I'm looking for a living and I never mix the two things in one. And if there's no childer sick nor sore, I care nothing else and if herself outside wants to go somewhere, I'm in the hope I can do it for her. A travelling man should be free to come and go as he wants and in my books the settled people has a small biteen of jealousy there.

'Of course a lot of travelling people brings trouble to their own doors. But why should us all be blackened by it? I suppose we're getting a small biteen of respect now. But we still can't insure a motor car and we have to go to the dole on separate days to the settled people, and the pubs won't serve us when you'd be looking to sit down and have a pint.'

We talk for a while about the suspicion between travellers and settled people and the necessity of setting up halting sites, whereby the travellers can continue to travel if they want. And the shameful absence of anti-discrimination law. There is no anger in his voice. No bitterness. An acceptance of the inevitability of Irish apartheid. The traveller's eldest son, John, speaks out.

'I think sometimes that we are treated like people from the third world. But the people of the third world has no choice but to live like the way they do. We have a choice, we want to live the way we want to live. But ye've forced us into a circle. We're the same as rats in a trap. And the rat will try and protect himself. And we are protecting ourselves. As best we can. We don't want AIDS, or abortions or divorce, or pushing injections in our arms.'

His is the voice of a younger generation, ever so slowly becoming politicised in a world largely indifferent to the plight of the traveller. The traveller hands one of the girls a cigarette. 'Light that for your father,' he sighs, without looking at her.

'A man said to me once, "Why don't you give up the fags, John?" And I said I'm a good while at them now. I'll keep smoking them. A man that's fond of smoke, it would do more harm for him to give them up than to keep smoking them. It depends on the luck you get, the straw you pick. But there's one thing sure, it's been proved since the world began, I'm going to die one way or the other. Just like yourself. God keep it from you. I won't give up the drink either. I go to no pubs, I'll get a bottle above in Ballymun and I'll sit there on the bunker and drink it. Neat vodka without water nor soda. That's my drink. Straight down the hatch. Raw from the bottle. For when you're drunk, you're out of this world and you're happy in your sleep, would you agree to that?'

The traveller smiles. He has few teeth, his bruised knuckles are tattooed with the word 'Love'. There are flecks of grey in his hair and beard, but he is older in his years. Soon we are standing in the yard again. Rain falls over the towers in Ballymun and the fields beyond to the airport where planes come and go, the air shuddering after them. In the yellow light from the roadway birds gather on the telegraph wires.

'I'll tell you a story. I came out of the dead house in Temple Street, a placeen there for small children, God bless us and I felt in the need for a glass of stout, so I went into a shop there, but I didn't get as far as the counter. "Sorry we don't serve ye people here" — and when I got shamed that way, what I done then, in the heel of the hunt — says I "I didn't come in for a drink sir, I came in for a packet of fags." "Well it makes no differ," says the man. "We can't serve ye people here." And I looked around me and standing beside me was a black man from the far end of Africa. "Yes, sir, what can I get you," says the barman. "A pint of ale," says the black man. "Sit down, sir, and I'll bring it to you," and it was brought down on a tray. And I wouldn't be served fags. And a drink was brought to that man in a tray.

'But I went back the day after and I knew what time they were changing staff. And I was clever enough in my own way. I went in and bought a newspaper and didn't I go down to a garage I knew and got the lend of a boilersuit. This is known fact. Put on a pair of glasses, you get an oul' pair of glasses for a couple of pound.

'In I goes, sat down. And I sat there reading me paper. And you know that I can't neither read nor write and that the paper knew more about me than I knew about the paper. "And what'll it be," says the man behind the counter, and I done what John Wayne done in that picture, *The Quiet Man*, because that picture was made in my country round Ballynoonan. 'A pint of black beer,' says I, and it was given up to me. I wanted to see what respect would I get, for I was gone in as a settled man, but what he didn't know was I was a travelling man and I was playing his part. I was classed as a settled man and they gave me the height of respect.'

His children stand around listening, laughing at the oft-told tale of their father besting the settled people. Then the traveller among his children waves goodbye, God speeding me and wishing me a bed in heaven.

He won the heart . . .

My son is sleeping. My newborn son. So still it seems he's not breathing at all. This evening I rushed to the hospital, shared the elevator with a frightened mouse. My wife sitting up in bed dressed in hospital blue.

'Your wife,' the doctor said, shaking his head. 'She's been on the phone for the last hour. I've never seen anybody so calm. She's going to have it before twelve.'

'Today or tomorrow, doctor?'

'What planet are you from? Today, of course.' Would I like to go to see the labour room, he asks.

'Does it have a view?'

'In twenty years of delivering children, nobody's ever asked me that. As a matter of fact, the room looks out onto the East River. Why do you ask?'

'Because that's where I'm going to be looking.'

'Yes, I forgot,' he says, 'New Age dad. Little squeamish?'

'A little.'

'Just make sure you stay out of the way.'

I remember when I told my brother I was to become a father he said, 'Well, you're not shooting blanks anyway.'

My wife's time has come. I'm smocked and masked. I feel like an extra in an episode of *Marcus Welby*. I hold her hand as the trolley rushes to the delivery room. We'd spent weeks at Le Ma's classes, breathing and hand holding, laughing like idiots. All forgotten now as primitive man takes over.

'Hurry up, for fuck's sakes.' I can't bear to see her in pain.

'How does it feel?' the doctor asks her.

'How do you think it feels?' she screams. 'Like there's an articulated truck up there.'

'The language I've heard here,' smiles another doctor, 'you wouldn't believe.'

'What's it like to give birth?' I'd asked a girlfriend once.

'Try sticking an umbrella up your arse and opening it,' she informed me. All I keep thinking as I watch my wife scream in pain is thank God I'm not a woman.

The East River changes from grey to black. Among tears and sweat and blood and screams and one savage punch to my privates, my son is born, screeching red and bald.

The nurse holds him above the scales. 'Well, he's got a great set of balls,' she says, slapping him on the backside.

'Just like his dad,' I joke. Nobody hears me. We hold each other's hands, choked by tears.

'Well done,' is all I can say to my brave, beautiful wife.

It seems I could never feel more love than at this moment. He sleeps there in his cradle under the window.

The sounds of a hospital at night: only I am awake. Her arm hangs over the side of the bed like a broken doll. Only the sound of their breathing, my wife and child.

Moonlight slides through the window. My finger in his tiny hand. This is a moment I will never forget. The two of them asleep and me awake here remembering a day with my father in Kildare.

He takes the chipped enamel bucket with the blue rim and a wooden handle. Into the summer's morning we walk by Fairywood. A little stream gurgles among the rushes at the roadside. My hand in his. It smells of cigarettes. He is whistling. I know that song.

The whistling gypsy came over the hill,
Down through the valley so shady,
He whistled and he sang 'til the green woods rang,
and he won the heart of a lady.

Among trees only the faintest whispering of wind. Far off in a galvanised shed, Paddy Byrne's dogs are barking madly. Leaves are falling on the water of the well.

His foot on a broken stone, pushing back the leaves at the edge of the bucket. If you fell in there you'd never be heard of again. Down in the black hole where Hell is and those creatures with long arms reaching out to grab you and pull you down into their black world.

He pushes the leaves to the side of the well, slaps water around in the bucket, throwing it out over the brambles, wetting them.

And the bucket filled to the brim and the uneven rhythm of his walk and the water staining the roadway and the side of his trousers. And whistling between his teeth and the sound of the guns in the Curragh across the summer morning fields and the squiggle of smoke from the chimney of my uncle's house above. A plane has left a trail of white over a cloudless blue sky. We stand for a moment. It seems as if all my life was a beautiful still morning in summer at that moment.

My wife stirs in her sleep. Now she wakes. 'What are you doing?' she asks.

'Just thinking.'

'About what?'

'Remembering. Pictures in my head.'

She comes and stands before the cradle of our sleeping boy. 'Our child,' she says.

And we both stand there for a long time taking in the wonder and the mystery and the beauty of these moments. And I think about my father and me and my son. And it all seems to make sense. This thing called my life.

Three years later, my daughter Romy was born. The day after her birth I wrote the following prayer for her. It is for both of my children, and for myself.

Prayer for my Daughter

You are born in love and pain, given to us for a short time only, before we must let you go again with love and pain. One day you'll come to know how close they are one to the other — You are a treasure, a blessing, a prayer's answer, a jig in my Irish soul. You are me. And I am you. You are both of us, the love of your mother and me.

Let me be worthy of you. Let me lead you to truth, to beauty, to the mystery of the universe. Be a comfort for you, be your rock, your refuge, your eejit, your scratching post, your kick the cat, your guide and teacher. Your truest friend.

Let me be open to your child's wisdom teaching me with your soul's innocence the true nature of things. Don't let me take you for granted. Let me always be myself and allow you always to be yourself without judgement — give you the key to my secret heart and not be afraid to show you who I really am, nor of who you really are. Give me the strength to be gone from you when I must go, and to be near you when you most need me.

Let me take your hand and help you to find your true path. There will be sorrow, for that is the way of the world; but out of suffering, joy can come too — the peacock swallows a poisoned thorn to grow the miracle of a feather.

You will ask me great questions, and sometimes I will not know the answer. Perhaps we are not meant to know some things, for that is life too. A seeking. It may be our only purpose here.

All things are changing always. Yesterday is dust. Tomorrow a dream. Our gift is now. And so, my sweet angel, may you know love and be loved in return. May you know truth and laughter and peace and happiness, and may the great spirit of the universe enfold you in his arms and keep you safe for always.

FILM LIST

EXCALIBUR (US 1981)
Dist: Orion Pictures, Producer: John
Boorman, Director: John Boorman
Cast: Nigel Terry, Helen Mirren,
Nicholas Clay, *Gabriel Byrne*,
Liam Neeson

REFLECTIONS (UK 1983)
Dist: Artificial Eye Film Company Ltd.,
Producer: David Deutsch and Kevin
Billington, Director: Kevin Billington,
Cast: *Gabriel Byrne*, Donal McCann,
Harriet Walter

THE KEEP (UK 1983)
Dist: Paramount Pictures, Producer:
Gene Kirkwood, Howard Koch Jr.,
Director: Michael Mann
Cast: Scott Glenn, Ian McKellen,
Gabriel Byrne

HANNAH K (France 1983)
Dist: Gaumont International, Producer:
Constantin Costa-Gavras, Director:
Constantin Costa-Gavras
Cast: Jill Clayburgh, *Gabriel Byrne*,
Jean Yanne

DEFENCE OF THE REALM (UK 1985)
Dist: Rank Film Dist. Ltd (UK), Warner
Bros (USA), Producer: Robin Douet,
Lynda Myles
Director: David Drury
Cast: *Gabriel Byrne*, Greta Scacchi

GOTHIC (UK 1986)
Dist: Virgin Vision (UK), Producer:
Penny Corke, Robert Fox, Director:
Ken Russell
Cast: *Gabriel Byrne*, Julian Sands,
Natasha Richardson

JULIA AND JULIA (Italy 1987)
Dist: Cinecom International Films,
Producer: Massimo Fichera, Director:
Peter Del Monte
Cast: Kathleen Turner, Sting,
Gabriel Byrne

SIESTA (US and UK 1987)
Dist: Lorimar (USA/video), Palace
Pictures (UK), Producer: Gary Kurfirst,
Director: Mary Lambert
Cast: Ellen Barkin, Isabella Rossellini,
Jodie Foster, *Gabriel Byrne*

A SOLDIER'S TALE (New Zealand 1988)
Dist: Atlantic Releasing Corporation
(USA), Producer: Larry Parr, Director:
Larry Parr
Cast: *Gabriel Byrne*, Marianne Basler,
Judge Reinhold

MILLER'S CROSSING (US 1990)
Dist: Twentieth Century Fox, Producer:
Ethan Coen, Director: Joel Coen
Cast: *Gabriel Byrne*, Albert Finney,
John Turturro

INTO THE WEST (Ireland, US 1992)
Dist: Miramax (USA), Producer:
Gabriel Byrne, Tim Palmer, Director:
Mike Newell
Cast: *Gabriel Byrne*, Ellen Barkin

COOL WORLD (US 1992)
Dist: Paramount Pictures,
Producer: Frank Mancuso Jr., Director:
Ralph Bakshi
Cast: *Gabriel Byrne*, Kim Basinger, Brad
Pitt

IN THE NAME OF THE FATHER
(US 1993)
Dist: Universal Pictures, Executive
Producer: *Gabriel Byrne*, Director: Jim
Sheridan

A DANGEROUS WOMAN (US 1993)
Dist: Gramercy Pictures, Producer:
Naomi Foner, Director: Stephan
Gyllenhaal
Cast: Barbara Hershey, Debra Winger,
Gabriel Byrne

POINT OF NO RETURN
(THE ASSASSIN) (US 1993)
Dist: Warner Bros (USA), Producer: Art
Linson, Director: John Badham
Cast: Bridget Fonda, *Gabriel Byrne*,
Dermot Mulroney, Anne Bancroft

TRIAL BY JURY (US 1994)
Dist: Warner Bros, Producer: James G.
Robinson, Director: Heywood Gould
Cast: William Hurt, *Gabriel Byrne*,
Joanne Whalley-Kilmer,
Armande Assante

A SIMPLE TWIST OF FATE (US 1994)
Dist: Buena Vista Distribution Co.,
(USA), Producer: Ric Kidney, Director:
Gillies MacKinnon
Cast: Steve Martin, *Gabriel Byrne*,
Catherine O'Hara, Stephen Baldwin

LITTLE WOMEN (US 1994)
Dist: Columbia Pictures,
Producer: Denise Denovi, Director:
Gillian Armstrong
Cast: Winona Ryder, *Gabriel Byrne*,
Susan Sarandon

USUAL SUSPECTS (US 1994)
Dist: Polygram Filmed Entertaining,
Spelling Films International, Producer:
Michael McDonnell
Director: Brian Singer
Cast: *Gabriel Byrne*, Chaz Palminteri,
Stephen Baldwin, Kevin Pollak, Kevin
Spacey, Pete Postlethwaite

FRANKIE STARLIGHT (Ireland 1994)
Producer: Noel Pearson, Director:
Michael Lindsey Hogg
Cast: Matt Dillon, Anne Parrilaud,
Gabriel Byrne

DEADMAN (US 1994)
Producer: Jim Jarmusch and Demetra
MacBride, Director: Jim Jarmusch
Cast: Johnny Depp, *Gabriel Byrne*,
Robert Mitchum

SMILLA'S SENSE OF SNOW
(1997 Fox Searchlight)
Producer: Bernd Eichinger, Martin
Mosszkowicz, Director: Bille August
Cast: Julia Ormond, *Gabriel Byrne*,
Richard Harris, Vanessa Redgrave,
Robert Loggia

LAST OF THE HIGH KINGS
(1998 Miramax)
Producer: Tim Palmer, Director: David
Keating, Screenplay: David Keating,
Gabriel Byrne
Cast: *Gabriel Byrne*, Jared Leto,
Christina Ricci, Catherine O'Hara,
Stephen Rea, Colm Meaney, Ciaran
Fitzgerald, Lorraine Pilkington, Emily
Mortimer, Jason Barry, Karl Hayden

THE END OF VIOLENCE
(1997 MGM Studio)
Producer: Deepak Nayar, Wim
Wenders, Nicholas Klein, Director:
Wim Wenders
Cast: *Gabriel Byrne*, Andie McDowell,
Bill Pullman, Daniel Benzali, Peter
Horton, Udo Kier, K. Todd Freeman,
John Diehl, Pruitt Taylor Vince, Loren
Dean, Traci Lind

THE MAN IN THE IRON MASK
(1998 United Artists Studio)
Producer: Russell Smith, Randall
Wallace, Director: Randall Wallace,
Cast: Gerard Depardieu, John
Malkovich, Jeremy Irons, Leonardo
DiCaprio, *Gabriel Byrne*, Judith
Godreche, Anne Parillaud, Edward
Atterton, Peter Sarsgaard

THE POLISH WEDDING
(1998 Fox Searchlight Studio)
Producers: Tom Rosenberg, Geoffrey
Stier, Julia Chasman, Director: Theresa
Connelly
Cast: Lena Olin, *Gabriel Byrne*, Claire
Danes, Mili Avital, Daniel Lapaine,
Adam Trese, Rade Serbedzija, Jeffrey
Nordling

STIGMATA (1999 MGM Studio)
Producer: Frank Mancuso Jr
Director: Rupert Glynn Wainwright
Cast: Patricia Arquette, *Gabriel Byrne*,
Patrick Muldoon, Nia Long, Jonathan
Pryce, Portia De Rossi

TELEVISION
'The Riordans' (RTE)
'Bracken' (RTE)
'Joyce in June' (BBC 1981)
'Treatment' (BBC 1981)
'Mussolini' (NBC 1982)
'Christopher Columbus' (CBS 1981)